CW01335931

The Lost Muse

The Collected Poems of Charlotte Mew

Edited by Stephen R. Pastore

Grand Oak Books
2014

GRAND OAK BOOKS

The Lost Muse: The Collected Poems of Charlotte Mew

Copyright 2014. All rights reserved. Printed in the United States of America. No part of this book may be used or reproduced in any manner whatsoever without prior written consent except in the case of brief quotations embodied in critical articles or reviews. For information, address Grand Oak Books.

Published by:
Grand Oak Books Publishing, Ltd

Library of Congress Cataloging-in-Publication Data:

Mew, Charlotte

For Heather

The Lost Muse

The Collected Poems of
Charlotte Mew

CONTENTS

Introduction..13
A Note on the Text..23
Song of Sorrow..27
The Wind and the Tree..28
The Farmer's Bride..29
At The Convent Gate..31
Requiescat...32
The Little Portress..34
Afternoon Tea..36
She Was A Sinner...37
Song..38
Fame..39
The Narrow Door...40
The Fête...41
Beside the Bed...46
In Nunhead Cemetery...47
The Pedlar..50
Pecheresse..51
The Changeling..53
Ken..56
A Quoi Bon Dire..59
The Quiet House..60
On the Asylum Road..63
Jour des Mortes..64
The Forest Road...65
Madeleine in Church..68
Exspecto Resurrectionem..74
On the Road to the Sea...75
The Sunlit House..77
The Shade-Catchers..78
Le Sacre-Coeur...79
Song...80
Saturday Market...81
Arracombe Wood...83
Sea Love..84
The Road to Kérity..85
I Have Been Through the Gates....................................86

The Cenotaph..87
In the Fields..88
From a Window..89
Not for that City..90
Rooms..91
Monsieur qui Passe...92
Do Dreams Lie Deeper?...94
Domus Caedet Arborem..95
Fin de Fête...96
Again..97
Epitaph..98
Friend, Wherefore-?...99
I So Like Spring..100
Here Lies a Prisoner..101
May, 1915..102
June, 1915..103
Ne Me Tangeto...104
Old Shepherd's Prayer..105
My Heart Is Lame..106
On Youth Struck Down..107
The Rambling Sailor...108
The Call...110
Absence..111
The Trees Are Down...112
Smile Death..114
To a Child in Death...115
Moorland Night...116
An Ending...117
A Question..119
Left Behind...120
A Farewell...121
"There Shall Be No Night There"...................................122
V.R.I..123
To a Little Child in Death..124
Peri en Mer...125
Unpublished Poems..127
Bibliography...129
Index..135

Introduction

Alida Klemantaski Monro, Harold's wife, wrote a brief biography of Charlotte Mew as an introduction to Mew's Collected Poems of 1953. She described her first meeting with Mew on 15 November, 1915 at Harold Monro's Poetry Bookshop in London at the behest of Harold who wanted to publish a book of Charlotte's poetry. He was greatly impressed with her poem, "The Farmer's Bride" when he read it in The Nation. The Poetry Bookshop had its own imprint and was forever on the search for new poetic talent. Mew responded to Harold's letter in a self-deprecating way and agreed to meet the two at the shop. Her greeting to Alida is now apocryphal: "Are you Charlotte Mew?," said Alida. "I am sorry to say I am," was Charlotte's reply. Some might consider this answer overly affectatious, but Alida felt, accurately, that Charlotte was genuine and really did not want to be within her own skin.

Of course, even a light perusal of her poetry would reveal the same truth. Charlotte Mew's sense of self-hate and an awareness of her differentness permeate her work. Her sense of not belonging, of a spiritual scarring, perhaps, seemed quite natural, as if this was the order of things, an order to which she had grown inured. Early in her relationship to Alida, Charlotte was "enigmatic"; Alida knew none of the facts of her background or her life story beyond what little she had heard by way of anecdotes from other Poetry Bookshop poets. Alida did know that Charlotte was in her midforties but had published very little in the way of poetry. What reputation she did have was based on her short stories and poems published in *The Yellow Book* in the 1890s. Quite clearly, though, it was her poetry that mattered most to Charlotte. Her style and content were unique for her time, although one can trace the threads of Christina Rossetti, Emily Bronte and even Emily Dickinson in her work. And certainly there was an affinity to Thomas Hardy whose many poems of loss and bereavement strike the same dissonant chord as her's. There are even traces of Ezra Pound, who had published one of her poems in *The Egoist*. Her uneven metrics, her intensity, her "cubist" lineation and her use of the poetic persona all belie a soul that she clearly repressed in daily life, a soul she no doubt feared would one day break loose, perhaps in the insanity that pervaded her family. There is a sense of someone nearly crushed by the weight of an unbearable inner defect. She can be effusive, sometimes too much so, in her feelings about nature and to the evanescence of human life on earth, but in the shadows always lurk death and madness, the twin spirits that forever haunted her.

Alida Monro was compelled to know more about this poet because her poems invited inquiry and speculation into the poet's private life. At times, Mew seemed perilously close to an unhealthy association with radical feminist movements of the day: she dressed in men's clothes, she never married, and she had no close male friends. She was a confidant of the feminist novelist May Sinclair and Charlotte's reputation suffered because of it. Sinclair apparently spread a rumor of Mew's attempt at a lesbian dalliance. She was rebuffed, according to Sinclair, who made no bones about spreading the tale. None of this could have helped Charlotte with her personal issues and her natural sense of privacy. On the other hand, she was compulsively moralistic and could not countenance even the appearance of an impropriety in others. Had Sinclair or any woman made overtures to her, she would have been shocked, no doubt. It is difficult to believe that the socially repressed Charlotte Mew would have risked public approbation for the sake of an infatuation with May Sinclair, but Charlotte often seemed compelled to do things that consciously she would never consider doing. Alida even felt that Charlotte was at times "two people" struggling for mastery over one life. Of course, Alida's hypothesis could have been based on her own studies of Darwinism as it was then being interpreted to explain such non-Darwinian concepts as sociopathology. Or, as Émile Zola put it, the struggle of the inner beast for control of the human soul.

In 1916, Charlotte's first book of poetry was published under the Poetry Bookshop imprint, *The Farmer's Bride*. This was a difficult time for the shop, its owner, its poets and the nation because the Great War was in full swing and devouring the young men of Europe at a furious pace (including some Poetry Bookshop poets like Rupert Brooke). Nonetheless, Charlotte threw herself apparently uncharacteristically into the publication of the book; she wrote numerous notes concerning cover design, the quality and color of the paper and revised several poems. She even provided a skeleton outline of a biography to Alida: Charlotte Mary Mew was born on 15 November, 1869 in London at 30 Doughty Street and was the daughter of a spendthrift architect, Frederick, and a pleasant diminutive mother named Anna Maria Kendall, who was the daughter of Frederick's business partner, H. E. Kendall. This couple produced seven children, Charlotte being the third. Two of her brothers died in infancy; another died at the age of five when Charlotte was seven. Of the four remaining children, her older brother Henry developed schizophrenia at the age of 22 and eventually was committed to a sanatorium in Peckham where he resided until the age of thirty-six when he died (in 1901). As children, Henry was Charlotte's protector and she never stopped looking up to him as more of a father than the fast-living Frederick who rarely showed any interest in his children. Frederick died of cancer in 1898, although it is perhaps indicative of the uncertainty of the details of Charlotte's life that at least one biographer, the renowned Louis Untermeyer, has him dying "when she was an infant." The loss of her father goes virtually unnoticed in her poems while the death or mental illness of her siblings is seminal to her work. Henry's fate particularly affected Charlotte and the pain she felt at his insanity and her loss of his guidance and companionship is a consistent thread in her poetry. Not long before he died, her younger sister Freda who was born in 1879, developed the same symptoms and was similarly sent away to an asylum where she lived for sixty years. Not only were these mad siblings an emotional drain on Charlotte but their financial upkeep depleted the modest Mew family resources forcing Charlotte, her remaining sibling Anne and her mother to live frugally, almost impoverished for many years, always attempting to keep up a gentile front, but resorting to ever smaller residences and the embarrassing necessity of taking in boarders to help defray the cost of living.

The tragic "waste" of the lives of Henry and Freda frequented itself in Charlotte's poetry and opened the door to doubt of her own conservative religious beliefs. What often appears to be a plea against the loneliness she felt (much in the nature of what today has been described as "survivor guilt") ultimately becomes an expression of a fear of insanity. So prominent was this fear (egged on by a rash of published books and articles on the new science of genetics again based on what would become known as "social Darwinism"), that both Charlotte and Anne vowed never to marry and thus avoid the passing on of the "madness gene" that both felt were within them. The question first arose early in Charlotte's adolescence when her mother's brother showed signs of schizophrenia. The perceived power of genes over her family led Charlotte, or at least one side of Charlotte, to pray for "godlessness;" much like Thomas Hardy, Charlotte reveals not so much an atheism or agnosticism as a belief that the "God of the Christians" or, indeed, of any organized religion, could not have created so imperfect and tragic a world. When she says, "I do not envy him his victories. His arms are full of broken things," she is praying for a different universe where a loving god would have no insanity, no poverty and no cruelty. In her desperate attempt at reconciling her own deep faith and the pain that surrounded her, she says, in "On the Asylum Road," that the mad inmates were "the incarnate wages of man's sin." Charlotte truly believed and feared that a passionate and untamed personality (like hers) was a disease or at least the symptoms of one. Her poems, therefore, alternate between a humanistic reverence of Christ and a deep-seated regret that there probably is no God. This sometimes confusing view of religion led one printing firm to refuse to typeset *The Farmer's Bride* because it seemed "blasphemous" to its Methodist typesetter (in particular, "Madeleine in Church").

Charlotte's few biographers have made a lesbian of her, but there is no evidence whatsoever that she was a lesbian or had any leanings in that direction. Charlotte has been claimed after death by feminist and gay activists who see in her plaintive poetry the suppressed victim of a gender crisis. Penelope Fitzgerald in *Charlotte Mew and Her Friends* made the assertion that while Charlotte was a lesbian, she never had a lesbian sexual encounter or any sexual encounter, for that matter. The gay activist agenda has singled out Charlotte (and many others) as a victim to a prejudice that never provably touched Charlotte. Her failure to marry has already been explained; her "queer garb" was actually quite *de rigueur* for artistic and literary women of the period (Charlotte herself said she got the idea of wearing a man's jacket from one of her much admired school teachers), like smoking was to Victorian women. It was the "Bohemian" look and lifestyle that evolved during the Aesthetic Movement in the 1890s. Artists like the Rossettis, Whistler, Stephen Crane, Oscar Wilde, all had a go at appearing anti-establishment. It might have been the first time in history that artists knowingly put on the uniform of a counter-culture.

Charlotte was pathologically shy and embarrassed of her lack of financial resources, her meagre surroundings and her dysfunctional family. Is it any wonder that someone with such pathologically low self-esteem would have no close male friends? The retro-analysts have seized upon these scant outward symptoms and have made a lesbian of her with not a shred of actual proof; no letters, poems, stories or confessions of the "love that dare not speak its name" are extant; most unusual for a writer. Charlotte Mew is mentioned and anthologized on over 15 lesbian/gay/feminist websites as of this writing. Whether or not Charlotte Mew was a lesbian is irrelevant to the appreciation of her poetry and discussions of it in that light add absolutely nothing. It is a "club" she would most assiduously have avoided.

In P[eggy]. B. Parris's interesting and inventive ficto-autobiographical novel *His Arms Are Full of Broken Things*, the author asserts not only that Charlotte had lesbian yearnings for three women in the course of her life, but was a secret lover of Thomas Hardy! Even after her death, "the god of broken things" has not let Charlotte rest in peace. This novel places Mew and Hardy together at the British Museum in 1892 (24 years before any record of their actual meeting) and has Charlotte carrying on another one of her unconsummated love affairs with him until Hardy's death in 1928. It seems that the most "broken thing" in this novel is the truth. In fact, Hardy respected Charlotte's poetry enough to copy out in his own hand (on the back of a British Museum Library slip) her poem "Fin de Fete." After Hardy's death in January 1928, Sidney Cockerell found the scrap in Hardy's desk and sent it to Charlotte, who treasured it. Cocerell mistakenly told Charlotte that this was the only poem not by him in his hand. Six months later, she gave it to Alida Monro just days before she committed suicide. Hardy could not have paid a greater compliment to a poet than he did with that scrap of paper.

In 1923, Charlotte was granted a Civil List Pension with the aid of Sidney Cockerell. This particular incident, the pension, has led to more misunderstanding than most of Charlotte's often misunderstood life. Cockerell introduced Charlotte's poetry to Thomas Hardy in 1918 or thereabouts. Hardy invited Charlotte to Max Gate and apparently gave her an open invitation to attend whenever she could. It was his way with others in his profession to leave his door unlocked for seekers of advice, succour or just a hot meal. All the biographers have quoted Hardy as saying she was "far and away the best living poet, who will be remembered when others are forgotten." In fact, what Hardy actually said (in writing, anyway) was that Charlotte was, "the greatest poetess I have come across just lately, in my judgment, though so meagre in her output." (In Hardy's day, saying someone was the "greatest female poet" would have been scant praise, something akin, perhaps, to saying a 5'6" man is the "best basketball player under 5'7"."). Like Parris, Alida Monro and Penelope Fitzgerald have attributed the Civil List Pension application wording to a private utterance of Hardy. In fact, John Masefield drafted the application at the behest of Cockerell, signed it, sent it along to Hardy who, of course, at the prodding of Cockerell, signed it as well (along with Poetry Bookshop's Walter de la Mare). Notwithstanding Hardy's earlier opinion, Masefield was probably correct in his assertion.

Charlotte revered her sister Anne. Anne was a painter by profession; not very successful as an artist, she earned her living painting decorative finishes (mostly flowers) on household items and furniture. She also did some minor art restoration to supplement the meagre living the Mews were left with after deductions for asylum bills. Both of them acted much the nursemaid for their frail and aging mother; when Anna Maria finally died in 1923, Charlotte and Anne no longer felt the need to spend their scant resources on a house and both moved into Anne's studio. Here they lived, Charlotte producing some poetry, Anne painting, for four years. In January of 1927 Anne was diagnosed with what now appears to have been liver cancer. Charlotte doted over Anne during the six months it took for the disease to conquer her. In June of 1927 Anne succumbed; Charlotte was beyond all consolation, even obsessing over a notion she had that one's relatives should open a vein in a deceased loved one to ensure against burial while still alive. Charlotte was certain that Anne might have been buried alive and never forgave herself for not taking this gruesome precaution. Alida Monro, ever the friend and one of the few people Charlotte felt truly at ease with, sought medical help for Charlotte. The doctors recommended putting Charlotte in an asylum, but Charlotte adamantly refused. Ultimately, she admitted herself to a dreary nursing home on Beaumont Street in London "for a rest and medical supervision." On March 24, 1928 Alida wrote that Charlotte's room was dismal, having a window that only looked out at a large brick wall; Charlotte would crane her neck to watch the pigeons land on the top of the wall against a faint sliver of blue sky; "she went out and bought a bottle of disinfectant [Lysol] and went back [to her room] and swallowed it." The corrosive effect of the poison was slow acting and while doctors tried various remedies like olive oil to slow or arrest the effects, Charlotte said her final words, "Don't keep me; let me go." Shortly before her death, Charlotte had inherited

£8000 from her mother's uncle; apparently not all the money in the world could have deterred Charlotte from the path fate had chosen.

The name of Charlotte Mew was not mentioned in the replies to contemporary critics who often asserted at the time that there had been no great "women-poets." She did not figure prominently or at all in the increasing numbers of books published shortly after her death dealing with contemporary verse. The several editions of her poems appearing over the decades since 1928 have all had short runs and have gone out of print within a year or two of their appearance. Nor is any of this surprising, since her total published output is only now up to 60 some-odd poems. And yet, if the half-a-dozen people whose views on poetry deserve respect were consulted, I think that they would have no doubt that Charlotte Mew deserves to be remembered. Her first book in its final form, *The Farmer's Bride* contained "Fame," and it ends:

> Yet, to leave Fame, still with such eyes and that bright hair!
> God! If I might! And before I go hence
> Take in her stead
> To our tossed bed
> One little dream, no matter how small, how wild
> Just now, I think, I found it in a field under a fence
> A frail new-born lamb, ghostly and pitiful and white,
> A blot upon the night
> The moon's dropped child.

Such a child of the moon was Charlotte Mew and just such is and will be her memory. She was very near to "the dark borders to which the moon waveringly points." She heard the anguish and the unknown happiness that is "unacquainted with the sun." She fled with "The Farmer's Bride:"

> Happy enough to chat and play
> With birds and rabbits and such as they,
> So long as men-folk keep away.

With the Circus-rider on her white horse, "She stood in the bright moonlight at the door of a strange room." She broke with the beloved dead, "into the odd, odd smile at this fraud of death." She had felt the heart of the changeling beat against hers:

I shall grow up, but never grow old,
I shall always, always be very cold,
I shall never come back again.

She had looked into her mad brother Henry's eyes which looked at you "as two red- wounded stars might do." And, while still sharing "the shadow of Life," she had passed through the gates and come back to weep over the empty heart "Like the heart of the holy city old, blind, beautiful Jerusalem,/ Over which Christ wept."

She was fifty-eight when she died. She had known much sorrow, and had been much, if narrowly, loved. It is not necessary to say more of this woman - her memory is safe with her friends, many born long after her death. Nor of this poet, because she has spoken for herself, and she will be heard always.

It is ironic that Charlotte Mew, at least to her biographers' eyes, needed more than her poetry to justify their study of her. Whether it was a fictional love affair with Thomas Hardy or his "effusive" praise, whether it was her "lesbian connection," or her particularly cruel suicide, Charlotte was never simply a poet who created great poetry. It is indicative of the vagueness surrounding Charlotte Mew that in the introduction to her second book of poetry published less than a year after her death, *The Rambling Sailor,* her closest friend, Alida Monro misstated Charlotte's birthday by a full year, that the number of her written poems were listed in one obituary as 28, that another called her Charlotte "New." Her discovered output is scant by standards of her day, but what a density of quality. Most biographers agree that she likely destroyed many poems before anyone saw them. Despite Sidney Cockerell's kind obituary where he stated that she will be "remembered long after others are forgotten," the real Charlotte Mew has been forgotten or, rather, lost. Her life and her poetry, indeed, have gone missing in the fog of time; hopefully, this book will help the world to find her.

A Note on the Text

It was not until the Poetry Bookshop published Charlotte Mew's poems in 1916, that her work ever appeared in book form. She was quite taken with the idea and took great pains in helping the Monro's with the physical appearance of the book, The Farmer's Bride. However, money was short and, due to the war, materials were shorter still. Harold Monro did try to produce a quality book, nonetheless, with what supplies were available to him. We have reproduced the cover illustration as a frontis, although Charlotte thought the artist, Claud Lovatt Fraser had not read the poems. We disagree; the attenuated farm house, with such a distorted distance between the ground and upper floors, certainly emphasizes the great psychological distance between the farmer and his wife. Charlotte wanted a green paper cover; all that could be found by Monro was grey. She also wanted her long lines to run on, but lack of paper prevented this. She was unconcerned with grammar and line punctuation, so we have attempted to duplicate the form of her poems from existing first editions of her work including misspelled place names. The first two poems, printed here for the first time under her true name originally appeared in The Yellow Book under her pen name, "Charles Catty." In a letter to Alida Monro, she revealed this in 1925. The Yellow Book published many of her short stories early in her career, but she was reluctant to have them publish her poems under her own name and, in fact, ceased all association with the journal after the Oscar Wilde scandal. This is all we now know of her input. We have given her what she wanted insofar as we know it to be. The green paper cover, the long lines unchopped, and we have relegated the Lovatt illustration to the frontis, more as a historical record than as a summary of the contents.

The Lost Muse:
The Collected Poems of Charlotte Mew

TO _____

*He asked life of thee, and thou gayest him a long life:
even for ever and ever..*

Song of Sorrow

I can sing not of youth or of morning;
I have ears for no music of bird;
I have eyes for no beauty adorning
The lives of young lovers.
One warning I bring you—one bitter cold word:
Sorrow, sorrow, I sing,
Sorrow, sorrow:
The woods echo—Sorrow, and echoing, say—
If it come not to-day,
Then—to-morrow.

I can sing not of love or of laughter;
These fail and are ended and die
As an echo beneath the wood's rafter
Swoons *off,* and is heard never after,
So love and so laughter wing by.
Sorrow, sorrow, I sing,
Sorrow, sorrow:
The years answer—Sorrow, and answering, say—
Ye who weep not to-day
Will to-morrow.

The Wind and the Tree

Sang the wind to the tree,
O be mournful with me:
There is nothing can last or can stay;
And the joy of new leaves
Turns to sorrow that grieves
The bare bough—on a day,
On a day.

Sang the tree to the wind,
Obe happy—I find
There is nothing time fails to restore
And the fall that bereaves,
Makes the joy of new leaves
In the spring—evermore,
Evermore.

The wind sighed to the tree,
Obe mournful with me:
Theleaves come not again that I blow;
And I mourn for the lives
No renewal revives,
The leaves fall'n—long ago,
Long ago.

The Farmer's Bride

Three Summers since I chose a maid,
Too young maybe—but more's to do
At harvest-time than bide and woo.
When us was wed she turned afraid
Of love and me and all things human;
Like the shut of a winter's day.
Her smile went out, and 'twasn't a woman—
More like a little frightened fay.
One night, in the Fall, she runned away.

"Out 'mong the sheep, her be," they said,
'Should properly have been abed;
But sure enough she wasn't there
Lying awake with her wide brown stare.
So over seven-acre field and up-along across the down
We chased her, flying like a hare
Before our lanterns. To Church-Town
All in a shiver and a scare
We caught her, fetched her home at last
And turned the key upon her, fast.

She does the work about the house
As well as most, but like a mouse:
Happy enough to chat and play
With birds and rabbits and such as they,
So long as men-folk keep away.
"Not near, not near!" her eyes beseech
When one of us comes within reach.
The women say that beasts in stall
Look round like children at her call.

The Lost Muse

I've hardly heard her speak at all.

Shy as a leveret, swift as he,
Straight and slight as a young larch tree,
Sweet as the first wild violets, she,
To her wild self. but what to me?

The short days shorten and the oaks are brown,
The blue smoke rises to the low grey sky,
One leaf in the still air falls slowly down,
A magpie's spotted feathers lie
On the black earth spread white with rime,
The berries redden up to Christmas-time.
What's Christmas-time without there be
Some other in the house than we!

She sleeps up in the attic there
Alone, poor maid! 'Tis but a stair
Betwixt us. Oh! my God! the down,
The soft young down of her, the brown,
The brown of her- her eyes, her hair, her hair!

At The Convent Gate

"Why do you shrink away, and start and stare?
Life frowns to see you leaning at death's gate—
Not back, but on. Ah! sweet, it is too late:
You cannot cast these kisses from your hair.
Will God's cold breath blow kindly anywhere
Upon such burning gold? Oh! lips worn white
With waiting! Love will blossom in a night
And you shall wake to find the roses there!"

"Oh hush! He seems to stir, He lifts His Head.
He smiles. Look where He hangs against the sky.
He never smiled nor stirred, that God of pain
With tired eyes and limbs above my bed—
But loose me, this is death, I will not die—
Not while He smiles. Oh! Christ, Thine own again!"

Requiescat

Your birds that call from tree to tree
Just overhead, and whirl and dart,
Your breeze fresh-blowing from the sea,
And your sea singing on, Sweetheart.

Your salt scent on the thin sharp air
Of this grey dawn's first drowsy hours,
While on the grass shines everywhere
The yellow starlight of your flowers.

Atthe road's end your strip of blue
Beyond that line of naked trees—
Strange that we should remember you
As if you would remember these!

As if your spirit, swaying yet
To the old passions, were not free
Of Spring's wild magic, and the fret
Of the wilder wooing of the sea!

What threat of old imaginings,
Half-haunted joy, enchanted pain,
Or dread of unfamiliar things
Should ever trouble you again?

Yet you would wake and want, you said
The little whirr of wings, the clear
Gay notes, the wind, the golden bed
Of the daffodil: and they are here!

Just overhead, they whirl and dart
Your birds that call from tree to tree,

Your sea is singing on- Sweetheart,
Your breeze is flowing from the sea.

Beyond the line of naked trees
At the road's end, your stretch of blue—
Strange if you should remember these
As we, ah! God! remember you!

The Little Portress
(St. Gilda de Rhuys)

The stillness of the sunshine lies
Upon her spirit: silence seems
To look out from its place of dreams
When suddenly she lifts her eyes
To waken, for a little space,
The smile asleep upon her face.

A thousand years of sun and shower,
The melting of unnumbered snows
Go to the making of the rose
Which blushes out its little hour.
So old is Beauty: in its heart
The ages seem to meet and part.

Like Beauty's self, she holds a clear
Deep memory of hidden things—
The music of forgotten springs—
So far she travels back, so near
She seems to stand to patient truth
As old as Age, as young as Youth.

That is her window, by the gate.
Now and again her figure flits
Across the wall. Long hours she sits
Within: on all who come to wait.
Her Saviour too is hanging there
A foot or so above her chair.

"Soeur Marie de l'enfant Jesus,"
You wrote it in my little book—
Your shadow-name. Your shadow-look

Is dimmer and diviner too,
But not to keep: it slips so far
Beyond us to that golden bar
Where angels, watching from their stair,
Half-envy you your tranquil days
Of prayer as exquisite as praise,—
Grey twilights softer than their glare
Of glory: all sweet human things
Which vanish with the whirr of wings.

Yet will you, when you wing your way
To whiter worlds, more whitely shine
Or shed a radiance more divine
Than here you shed from day to day—
    High in His heaven a quiet star,
Be nearer God than now you are?

Afternoon Tea

Please you, excuse me, good five-o'clock people,
I've lost my last hatful of words,
And my heart's in the wood up above the church steeple,
I'd rather have tea with the birds.

Gay Kate's stolen kisses, poor Barnaby's scars,
John's losses and Mary's gains,
Oh! what do they matter, my dears, to the stars
Or the glow-worms in the lanes!

I'd rather lie under the tall elm-trees,
With old rooks talking loud overhead,
To watch a red squirrel run over my knees,
Very still on my brackeny bed.

And wonder what feathers the wrens will be taking
For lining their nests next Spring;
Or why the tossed shadow of boughs in a great wind shaking
Is such a lovely thing.

She Was A Sinner

Love was my flower, and before He came—
"Master, there was a garden where it grew
Rank, with the colour of a crimson flame,
Thy flower too, but knowing not its name
Nor yet that it was Thine, I did not spare
But tore and trampled it and stained my hair,
My hands, my lips, with the red petals; see,
Drenched with the blood of Thy poor murdered flower
I stood, when suddenly the hour
Struck for me,
And straight I came and wound about Thy Feet
The strands of shame
Twinedwith those broken buds: till lo, more sweet,
More red, yet still the same,
Bright burning blossoms sprang around Thy brow
Beneath the thorns (I saw, I knew not how
The crown which Thou wast afterward to wear
On that immortal Tree)
And I went out and found my garden very bare,
But swept and watered it, then followed Thee.

There was another garden where to seek
Thee, first, I came in those grey hours
Of the Great Dawn, and knew Thee not till Thou didst speak
My name, that 'Mary' like a flash of light
Shot from Thy lips. Thou wast 'the gardener' too,
And then I knew
That evermore our flowers,
Thine, Lord, and mine, shall be a burning white."

Song

Oh! Sorrow, Sorrow, scarce I knew
Your name when, shaking down the may
In sport, a little child, I grew
Afraid to find you at my play.
I heard it ere I looked at you;
You sang it softly as you came
Bringing your little boughs of yew
To fling across my gayest game.

Oh! Sorrow, Sorrow, was I fair
That when I decked me for a bride,
You met me stepping down the stair
And led me from my lover's side?
Was I so dear you could not spare
The maid to love, the child to play,
But coming always unaware,
Must bid and beckon me away?

Oh! Sorrow, Sorrow, is my bed
So wide and warm that you must lie
Upon it; toss your weary head
And stir my slumber with your sigh?

I left my love at your behest,
I waved your little boughs of yew,
But, Sorrow, Sorrow, let me rest,
For oh! I cannot sleep with you!

Fame

Sometimes in the over-heated house, but not for long,
Smirking and speaking rather loud,
I see myself among the crowd,
Where no one fits the singer to his song,
Or sifts the unpainted from the painted faces
Of the people who are always on my stair;
They were not with me when I walked in heavenly places;
But could I spare
In the blind Earth's great silences and spaces,
The din, the scuffle, the long stare
If I went back and it was not there?
Back to the old known things that are the new,
The folded glory of the gorse, the sweet-briar air,
To the larks that cannot praise us, knowing nothing of what we do
And the divine, wise trees that do not care
Yet, to leave Fame, still with such eyes and that bright hair!
God! If I might! And before I go hence
Take in her stead
To our tossed bed,
One little dream, no matter how small, how wild.
Just now, I think I found it in a field, under a fence—
A frail, dead, new-born lamb, ghostly and pitiful and white,
A blot upon the night,
The moon's dropped child!

The Narrow Door

The narrow door, the narrow door
On the three steps of which the café children play
Mostly at shop with pebbles from the shore,
It is always shut this narrow door
But open for a little while to-day.

And round it, each with pebbles in his hand,
A silenced crowd the café children stand
To see the long box jerking down the bend
Of twisted stair; then set on end,
Quite filling up the narrow door
Till it comes out and does not go in any more.

Along the quay you see it wind,
The slow black line. Someone pulls up the blind
Of the small window just above the narrow door—
"Tiens! que veux-tu acheter?" Renée cries,
"Mais, pour quat Thus, des oignons, "Jean replies
And one pays down with pebbles from the shore.

The Fête

To-night again the moon's white mat
Stretches across the dormitory floor
While outside, like an evil cat
The *pion* prowls down the dark corridor,
Planning, I know, to pounce on me, in spite
For getting leave to sleep in town last night.
But it was none of us who made that noise,
      Only the old brown owl that hoots and flies
Out of the ivy—he will say it was us boys—
      Seigneur mon Dieu! the *sacré* soul of spies!
    He would like to catch each dream that lies
            Hidden behind our sleepy eyes:
Their dream~ But mine—it is the moon and the wood that sees;
All my long life how I shall hate the trees!

In the *Place d'Armes,* the dusty planes, all Summer through
Dozed with the market women in the sun and scarcely stirred
    To see the quiet things that crossed the Square—,
A tiny funeral, the flying shadow of a bird,
      The hump-backed barber Célestin Lemaire,
        Old madame Michel in her three-wheeled chair,
          And filing past to Vespers, two and two,
            The *demoiselles* of the *pensionnat.*
Towed like a ship through the harbour bar
        Safe into port, where *le petit Jesus*
Perhaps makes nothing of the look they shot at you:
      Si, c 'est defendu, mais que voulez-vous?
It was the sun. The sunshine weaves
A pattern on dull stones: the sunshine leaves
        The portraiture of dreams upon the eyes
          Before it dies:
        All Summer through
The dust hung white upon the drowsy planes

Till suddenly they woke with the Autumn rains.

      It is not only the little boys
        Who have hardly got away from toys,
But I, who am seventeen next year,
Some nights, in bed, have grown cold to hear
        That lonely passion of the rain
Which makes you think of being dead,
And of somewhere living to lay your head
        As if you were a child again,
Crying for one thing, known and near
Your empty heart, to still the hunger and the fear
     That pelts and beats with it against the pane.
     But I remember smiling too

At all the sun's soft tricks and those Autumn dreads
In winter time, when the grey light broke slowly through
The frosted window-lace to drag us shivering from our beds.
And when at dusk the singing wind swung down
Straight from the stars to the dark country roads
Beyond the twinkling town,
Striking the leafless poplar boughs as he went by,
Like some poor, stray dog by the wayside lying dead,
We left behind us the old world of dread,
I and the wind as we strode whistling on under the Winter sky.

And then in Spring for three days came the Fair
Just as the planes were starting into bud
Above the caravans: you saw the dancing bear
Pass on his chain; and heard the jingle and the thud.
Only four days ago
They let you out of this dull show
To slither down the *montagne russe* and chaff the man *a la tête de veau*—
Hit, slick, the bull's eye at the *tir,*
Spin round and round till your head went queer
On *the porcs-roulants. Oh! la~la! la fête!*
Va pour du vin, et le tête-a-tête

With the girl who sugars the *gaufres! Pauvrette,*
How thin she was; but she smiled, you bet,
As she took your tip—"One does not forget
The good days, Monsieur." Said with a grace,
But *sacrébleu!* what a ghost of a face!
And no fun too for the *demoiselles*
Of the *pensionnat,* who were hurried past,
With their *"Oh, que c'est beau—Ah, qu 'elle est belle!"*
A lap-dog's life from first to last!
The good nights are not made for sleep, nor the good days for dreaming in,
And at the end in the big Circus tent we sat and shook and stewed like sin!

Some children there had got—but where?
Sent from the south, perhaps—a red bouquet
Of roses, sweetening the fetid air
With scent from gardens by some far away blue bay.
They threw one at the dancing bear;
The white clown caught it. From St Rémy's tower
The deep, slow bell tolled out the hour;
The black clown, with his dirty grin
Lay, sprawling in the dust, as She rode in.

She stood on a white horse—and suddenly you saw the bend
Of a far-off road at dawn, with knights riding by,
A field of spears—and then the gallant day
Go out in storm, with ragged clouds low down, sullen and grey
Against red heavens: wild and awful, such a sky
As witnesses against you at the end
Of a great battle; bugles blowing, blood and dust—
The old *Morte d'Arthur,* fight you must—.
It died in anger. But it was not death
That had you by the throat, stopping your breath.
She looked like Victory. She rode my way.

She laughed at the black clown and then she flew
A bird above us, on the wing
Of her white arms; and you saw through

A rent in the old tent, a patch of sky
With one dim star. She flew, but not so high—
And then she did not fly;
She stood in the bright moonlight at the door
Of a strange room, she threw her slippers to the floor—
Again, again
You heard the patter of the rain,
The starving rain—it was this Thing,
Summer was this, the gold mist in your eyes;—
Oh God! it dies,
But after death—,
To-night the splendour and the sting
Blows back and catches at your breath,
The smell of beasts, the smell of dust, the scent of all the roses in the world, the sea, the Spring,
The beat of drums, the pad of hoofs, music, the dream, the dream, the Enchanted Thing!

At first you scarcely saw her face,
You knew the maddening feet were there
What called was that half-hidden, white unrest
To which now and then she pressed
Her finger tips; but as she slackened pace
And turned and looked at you it grew quite bare:
There was not anything you did not dare:—
Like trumpeters the hours passed until the last day of the Fair.

In the *Place d'Armes* all afternoon
The building birds had sung "Soon, soon,"
The shuttered streets slept sound that night,
It was full moon:
The path into the wood was almost white,
The trees were very still and seemed to stare:
Not far before your soul the Dream flits on,
But when you touch it, it is gone
And quite alone your soul stands there.

Mother of Christ, no one has seen your eyes: how can men pray
Even unto you?
There were only wolves' eyes in the wood—
My Mother is a woman too:
Nothing is true that is not good,
With that quick smile of hers, 1 have heard her say;—
I wish I had gone back home to-day;
I should have watched the light that so gently dies
From our high window, in the Paris skies,
The long, straight chain
Of lamps hung out along the Seine:
1 would have turned to her and let the rain
Beat on her breast as it does against the pane;—
Nothing will be the same again;—
There is something strange in my little Mother's eyes,
There is something new in the old heavenly air of Spring—
The smell of beasts, the smell of dust—The *Enchanted Thing!*

All my life long I shall see moonlight on the fern
And the black trunks of trees. Only the hair
Of any woman can belong to God.
The stalks are cruelly broken where we trod,
There had been violets there,
I shall not care
As I used to do when I see the bracken burn.

Beside the Bed

Someone has shut the shining eyes, straightened and folded
The wandering hands quietly covering the unquiet breast:
So, smoothed and silenced you lie, like a child, not again to be questioned or scolded;
But, for you, not one of us believes that this is rest.

Not so to close the windows down can cloud and deaden
The blue beyond: or to screen the wavering flame subdue its breath:
Why, if I lay my cheek to your cheek, your grey lips, like dawn, would quiver and redden,
Breaking into the old, odd smile at this fraud of death.

Because all night you have not turned to us or spoken
It is time for you to wake; your dreams were never very deep:
I, for one, have seen the thin, bright, twisted threads of them dimmed suddenly and broken,
This is only a most piteous pretence of sleep!

In Nunhead Cemetery

It is the clay that makes the earth stick to his spade;
He fills in holes like this year after year;
The others have gone; they were tired, and half afraid
But I would rather be standing here;

There is nowhere else to go. I have seen this place
From the windows of the train that's going past
Against the sky. This is rain on my face—
It was raining here when I saw it last.

There is something horrible about a flower;
This, broken in my hand, is one of those
He threw in just now: it will not live another hour;
There are thousands more: you do not miss a rose.

One of the children hanging about
Pointed at the whole dreadful heap and smiled
This morning, after THAT was carried out;
There is something terrible about a child.

We were like children, last week, in the Strand;
That was the day you laughed at me
Because I tried to make you understand
The cheap, stale chap I used to be
Before I saw the things you made me see.

This is not a real place; perhaps by-and-by
I shall wake—I am getting drenched with all this rain:
To-morrow I will tell you about the eyes of the Crystal Palace train
Looking down on us, and you will laugh and I shall see what you see again.

Not here, not now. We said "Not yet

The Lost Muse

Across our low stone parapet
Will the quick shadows of the sparrows fall."

But still it was a lovely thing
Through the grey months to wait for Spring
With the birds that go a-gypsying
In the parks till the blue seas call.
And next to these, you used to care
For the lions in Trafalgar Square,
Who'll stand and speak for London when her bell of Judgment tolls—
And the gulls at Westminster that were
The old sea-captains' souls.
To-day again the brown tide splashes, step by step, the river stair,
And the gulls are there!

By a month we have missed our Day:
The children would have hung about
Round the carriage and over the way
As you and I came out.

We should have stood on the gulls' black cliffs and heard the sea
And seen the moon's white track,
I would have called, you would have come to me
And kissed me back.

You have never done that: I do not know
Why I stood staring at your bed
And heard you, though you spoke so low,
But could not reach your hands, your little head.
There was nothing we could not do, you said,
And you went, and I let you go!

Now I will burn you back, I will burn you through,
Though I am damned for it we two will lie
And burn, here where the starlings fly
To these white stones from the wet sky—;
Dear, you will say this is not I—

It would not be you, it would not be you!

If for only a little while
You will think of it you will understand,
If you will touch my sleeve and smile
As you did that morning in the Strand
I can wait quietly with you
Or go away if you want me to— God! What is God? but your face has gone and your hand!
Let me stay here too.

When I was quite a little lad
At Christmas time we went half mad
For joy of all the toys we had,
And then we used to sing about the sheep
The shepherds watched by night;
We used to pray to Christ to keep
Our small souls safe till morning light—;
I am scared, I am staying with you to-night—
Put me to sleep.

I shall stay here: here you can see the sky;
The houses in the streets are much too high;
There is no one left to speak to there;
Here they are everywhere,
And just above them fields and fields of roses lie—
If he would dig it all up again they would not die.

The Pedlar

Lend me, a little while, the key
That locks your heavy heart, and I'll give you back—
Rarer than books and ribbons and beads bright to see,
This little Key of Dreams out of my pack.

The road, the road, beyond men's bolted doors,
There shall I walk and you go free of me,
For yours lies North across the moors,
And mine South. To what sea?

How if we stopped and let our solemn selves go by,
While my gay ghost caught and kissed yours, as ghosts don't do,
And by the wayside this forgotten you and I
Sat, and were twenty-two?

Give me the key that locks your tired eyes,
And I will lend you this one from my pack,
Brighter than coloured beads and painted books that make men wise:
Take it. No, give it back!

Pecheresse

Down the long quay the slow boats glide,
While here and there a house looms white
Against the gloom of the waterside,
And some high window throws a light
As they sail out into the night.

At dawn they will bring in again
To women knitting on the quay
Who wait for him, their man of men;
I stand with them, and watch the sea
Which may have taken mine from me.

Just so the long days come and go.
The nights, ma Doué! the nights are cold!
Our Lady's heart is as frozen snow,
Since this one sin I have not told;
And I shall die or perhaps grow old

Before he comes. The foreign ships
Bring many a one of face and name
As strange as his, to buy your lips,
A gold piece for a scarlet shame
Like mine. But mine was not the same.

One night was ours, one short grey day
Of sudden sin, unshrived, untold.
He found me, and I lost the way
To Paradise for him. I sold
My soul for love and not for gold.

He bought my soul, but even so,
My face is all that he has seen
His is the only face I know,
And in the dark church, like a screen,

It shuts God out; it comes between;

While in some narrow foreign street
Or loitering on the crowded quay,
Who knows what others he may meet
To turn his eyes away from me?
Many are fair to such as he!

There is but one for such as I
To love, to hate, to hunger for;
I shall, perhaps, grow old and die,
With one short day to spend and store,
One night, in all my life, no more.

Just so the long days come and go,
Yet this one sin I will not tell
Though Mary's heart is as frozen snow
And all nights are cold for one warmed too well.
But, oh! ma Doué! *the nights of Hell!*

The Changeling

Toll no bell for me, dear Father, dear Mother,
Waste no sighs;
There are my sisters, there is my little brother
Who plays in the place called Paradise,
Your children all, your children for ever;
But I, so wild,
Your disgrace, with the queer brown face, was never,
Never, I know, but half your child!

In the garden at play, all day, last summer,
Far and away I heard
The sweet "tweet-tweet" of a strange new-corner,
The dearest, clearest call of a bird.
It lived down there in the deep green hollow,
My own old home, and the fairies say
The word of a bird is a thing to follow,
So I was away a night and a day.

One evening, too, by the nursery fire,
We snuggled close and sat round so still,
When suddenly as the wind blew higher,
Something scratched on the window-sill.
A pinched brown face peered in—I shivered;
No one listened or seemed to see;
The arms of it waved and the wings of it quivered,
Whoo—I knew it had come for me;
Some are as bad as bad can be!
All night long they danced in the rain,
Round and round in a dripping chain,
Threw their caps at the window-pane,
Tried to make me scream and shout
And fling the bedclothes all about:

I meant to stay in bed that night,
And if only you had left a light
They would never have got me out.

Sometimes I wouldn't speak, you see,
Or answer when you spoke to me,
Because in the long, still dusks of Spring
You can hear the whole world whispering;
The shy green grasses making love,
The feathers grow on the dear, grey dove,
The tiny heart of the redstart beat,
The patter of the squirrel's feet,
The pebbles pushing in the silver streams,
The rushes talking in their dreams,
The swish-swish of the bat's black wings,
The wild-wood bluebell's sweet ting-tings,
Humming and hammering at your ear,
Everything there is to hear
In the heart of hidden things,
But not in the midst of the nursery riot,
That's why I wanted to be quiet,
Couldn't do my sums, or sing,
Or settle down to anything.
And when, for that, I was sent upstairs
I *did* kneel down to say my prayers;
But the King who sits on your high church steeple
Has nothing to do with us fairy people!

'Times I pleased you, dear Father, dear Mother,
Learned all my lessons and liked to play,
And dearly I loved the little pale brother
Whom some other bird must have called away.
Why did They bring me here to make me
Not quite bad and not quite good,
Why, unless They're wicked, do They want, in spite, to take me
Back to their wet, wild wood?
Now, every night I shall see the windows shining,

The gold lamp's glow, and the fire's red gleam,
While the best of us are twining twigs and the rest of us are whining
In the hollow by the stream.
Black and chill are Their nights on the wold;
And They live so long and They feel no pain:
I shall grow up, but never grow old,
I shall always, always be very cold,
I shall never come back again!

Ken

The town is old and very steep,
A place of bells and cloisters and grey towers,
And black clad people walking in their sleep—
A nun, a priest, a woman taking flowers
To her new grave; and watched from end to end
By the great Church above, through the still hours:
But in the morning and the early dark
The children wake to dart from doors and call
Downthe wide, crooked street, where, at the bend,
Before it climbs up to the park,
Ken's is the gabled house facing the Castle wall.

When first I came upon him there
Suddenly, on the half-lit stair,
I think I hardly found a trace
Of likeness to a human face
In his. And I said then
If in His image God made men,
Some other must have made poor Ken—
But for his eyes which looked at you
As two red, wounded stars might do.

He scarcely spoke, you scarcely heard,
His voice broke off in little jars
To tears sometimes. An uncouth bird
He seemed as he ploughed up the street,
Groping, with knarred, high-lifted feet
And arms thrust out as if to beat
Always against a threat of bars.

And oftener than not there'd be
A child just higher than his knee

Trotting beside him. Through his dim
Long twilight this, at least, shone clear,
That all the children and the deer,
Whom every day he went to see
Out in the park, belonged to him.

"God help the folk that next him sits
He fidgets so, with his poor wits."
The neighbours said on Sunday nights
When he would go to Church to "see the lights!"
Although for these he used to fix
His eyes upon a crucifix
In a dark corner, staring on
Till everybody else had gone.
And sometimes, in his evil fits,
You could not move him from his chair—
You did not look at him as he sat there,
Biting his rosary to bits.
While pointing to the Christ he tried to say
"Take it away."

Nothing was dead:
He said "a bird" if he picked up a broken wing,
A perished leaf or any such thing
Was just "a rose"; and once when I had said
He must not stand and knock there any more,
He left a twig on the mat outside my door.

Not long ago
The last thrush stiffened in the snow,
While black against a sullen sky
The sighing pines stood by.
But now the wind has left our rattled pane
To flutter the hedge-sparrow's wing,
The birches in the wood are red again
And only yesterday
The larks went up a little way to sing

The Lost Muse

What lovers say
Who loiter in the lanes to-day;
The buds begin to talk of May
With learned rooks on city trees,
And if God please
With all of these
We too, shall see another Spring.

But in that red brick barn upon the hill
I wonder—can one own the deer,
And does one walk with children still
As one did here—
Do roses grow
Beneath those twenty windows in a row—
And if some night
When you have not seen any light
They cannot move you from your chair
What happens there?
I do not know.

So, when they took
Ken to that place, I did not look
After he called and turned on me
His eyes. These I shall see—

A Quoi Bon Dire

Seventeen years ago you said
Something that sounded like Good-bye;
And everybody thinks that you are dead,
But I.

So I, as I grow stiff and cold
To this and that say Good-bye too;
And everybody sees that I am old
But you.

And one fine morning in a sunny lane
Some boy and girl will meet and kiss and swear
That nobody can love their way again
While over there
You will have smiled, I shall have tossed your hair.

The Quiet House

When we were children old Nurse used to say
The house was like an auction or a fair
Until the lot of us were safe in bed.
It has been quiet as the country-side
Since Ted and Janey and then Mother died
And Tom crossed Father and was sent away.
After the lawsuit he could not hold up his head,
Poor Father, and he does not care
For people here, or to go anywhere.

To get away to Aunt's for that week-end
Was hard enough; (since then, a year ago,
He scarcely lets me slip out of his sight—)
At first I did not like my cousin's friend,
I did not think I should remember him:
His voice has gone, his face is growing dim
And if I like him now I do not know.
He frightened me before he smiled—
He did not ask me if he might—
He said that he would come one Sunday night,
He spoke to me as if I were a child.

No year has been like this that has just gone by;
It may be that what Father says is true,
If things are so it does not matter why:
But everything has burned, and not quite through.
The colours of the world have turned
To flame, the blue, the gold has burned
In what used to be such a leaden sky.
When you are burned quite through you die.

Red is the strangest pain to bear;

In Spring the leaves on the budding trees;
In Summer the roses are worse than these,
More terrible than they are sweet:
A rose can stab you across the street
Deeper than any knife:
And the crimson haunts you everywhere—
Thin shafts of sunlight, like the ghosts of reddened swords have struck our stair
As if, coming down, you had spilt your life.

I think that my soul is red
Like the soul of a sword or a scarlet flower:
But when these are dead
They have had their hour.
I shall have had mine, too,
For from head to feet,
I am burned and stabbed half through,
And the pain is deadly sweet.

The things that kill us seem
Blind to the death they give:
It is only in our dream
The things that kill us live.

The room is shut where Mother died,
The other rooms are as they were,
The world goes on the same outside,
The sparrows fly across the Square,
The children play as we four did there,
The trees grow green and brown and bare,
The sun shines on the dead Church spire,
And nothing lives here but the fire,
While Father watches from his chair
Day follows day
The same, or now and then, a different grey,
Till, like his hair,
Which Mother said was wavy once and bright,

They will all turn white.

To-night I heard a bell again—
Outside it was the same mist of fine rain,
The lamps just lighted down the long, dim street,
No one for me— I think it is myself I go to meet:
I do not care; some day I *shall* not think; I shall not *be!*

On the Asylum Road

Theirs is the house whose windows—every pane—
Are made of darkly stained or clouded glass:
Sometimes you come upon them in the lane,
The saddest crowd that you will ever pass.
But still we merry town or village folk
Throw to their scattered stare a kindly grin,
And think no shame to stop and crack a joke
With the incarnate wages of man's sin.

None but ourselves in our long gallery we meet,
The moor-hen stepping from her reeds with dainty feet,
The hare-bell bowing on its stem,
Dance not with us; their pulses beat
To fainter music; nor do we to them
Make their life sweet.

The gayest crowd that they will ever pass
Are we to brother-shadows in the lane:
Our windows, too, are clouded glass
To them, yes, every pane!

Jour des Mortes
(Cimetière Montparnasse.)

Sweetheart, is this the last of all our posies
And little festivals, my flowers are they
But white and wistful ghosts of gayer roses
Shut with you in this grim garden? Not to-day,
Ah! no! come out with me before the grey gate closes
It is your fête and here is your bouquet!

The Forest Road

The forest road
The infinite straight road stretching away
World without end: the breathless road between the walls
Of the black listening trees: the hushed, grey road
Beyond the window that you shut to-night
Crying that you would look at it by day—
There is a shadow there that sings and calls
But not for you. Oh! hidden eyes that plead in sleep
Against the lonely dark, if I could touch the fear
And leave it kissed away on quiet lids—
If I could hush these hands that are half-awake,
Groping for me in sleep I could go free.
I wish that God would take them out of mine
And fold them like the wings of frightened birds
Shot cruelly down, but fluttering into quietness so soon.
Broken, forgotten things; there is no grief for them in the green Spring
When the new birds fly back to the old trees.
But it shall not be so with you. I will look back. I wish I knew that God would stand
Smiling and looking down on you when morning comes,
To hold you, when you wake, closer than I,
So gently though: and not with famished lips or hungry arms:
He does not hurt the frailest, dearest things
As we do in the dark. See, dear, your hair—
I must unloose this hair that sleeps and dreams
About my face, and clings like the brown weed
To drowned, delivered things, tossed by the tired sea
Back to the beaches. Oh! your hair! If you had lain
A long time dead on the rough, glistening ledge
Of some black cliff, forgotten by the tide,

The raving winds would tear, the dripping brine would rust away
Fold after fold of all the loveliness
That wraps you round, and makes you, lying here,
The passionate fragrance that the roses are.
But death would spare the glory of your head
In the long sweetness of the hair that does not die:
The spray would leap to it in every storm,
The scent of the unsilenced sea would linger on
In these dark waves, and round the silence that was you—
Only the nesting gulls would hear—but there would still be whispers in your hair;
Keep them for me; keep them for me. What *is* this singing on the road
That makes all other music like the music in a dream—
Dumb to the dancing and the marching feet; you know, in dreams, you see
Old pipers playing that you cannot hear,
And ghostly drums that only seem to beat. This seems to climb:
Is it the music of a larger place? It makes our room too small: it is like a stair,
A calling stair that climbs up to a smile you scarcely see,
Dim, but so waited for; and *you* know what a smile is, how it calls,
How if I smiled you always ran to me.
Now you must sleep forgetfully, as children do.
There is a Spirit sits by us in sleep
Nearer than those who walk with us in the bright day.
I think he has a tranquil, saving face: I think he came
Straight from the hills: he may have suffered there in time gone by,
And once, from those forsaken heights, looked down
Lonely himself, on all the lonely sorrows of the earth.
It is his kingdom—Sleep. If I could leave you there—
If, without waking you, I could get up and reach the door—!
We used to go together. —Shut, scared eyes,
Poor, desolate, desperate hands, it is not I
Who thrust you off. No, take your hands away—
I cannot strike your lonely hands. Yes, I have struck your heart,
It did not come so near. Then lie you there
Dear and wild heart behind this quivering snow

With two red stains on it: and I will strike and tear
Mine out, and scatter it to yours. Oh! throbbing dust,
You that were life, our little wind-blown hearts!
The road! the road!
There is a shadow there: I see my soul,
I hear my soul, singing among the trees!

Madeleine in Church

Here, in the darkness, where this plaster saint Stands nearer than God stands to our distress,
And one small candle shines, but not so faint As the far lights of everlastingness
I'd rather kneel than over there, in open day
Where Christ is hanging, rather pray
To something more like my own clay,
Not too divine;
For, once, perhaps my little saint
Before he got his niche and crown,
Had one short stroll about the town;
It brings him closer, just that taint
And anyone can wash the paint
Off our poor faces, his and mine!
Is that why I see Monty now? equal to any saint, poor boy, as good as gold,
But still, with just the proper trace
Of earthliness on his shining wedding face;
And then gone suddenly blank and old
The hateful day of the divorce:
Stuart got his, hands down, of course
crowing like twenty cocks and grinning like a horse:
But Monty took it hard. All said and done I liked him best,—
He was the first, he stands out clearer than the rest.
It seems too funny all we other rips
Should have immortal souls; Monty and Redge quite damnably
Keep theirs afloat while we go down like scuttled ships.—
It's funny too, how easily we sink,
One might put up a monument, I think
To half the world and cut across it "Lost at Sea!"
I should drown Jim, poor little sparrow, if I netted him to-night—
No, it's no use this penny light—
Or my poor saint with his tin-pot crown—
The trees of Calvary are where they were,
When we are sure that we can spare
The tallest, let us go and strike it down
And leave the other two still standing there.
I, too, would ask him to remember me
If there were any Paradise beyond this earth that I could see.

Oh! quiet Christ who never knew
The poisonous fangs that bite us through
And make us do the things we do,
See how we suffer and fight and die,
How helpless and how low we lie,
God holds You, and You hang so high,
Though no one looking long at You,
Can think you do not suffer too,
But, up there, from your still, star-lighted tree
What can You know, what can You really see
Of this dark ditch, the soul of me!

We are what we are: when I was half a child I could not sit
Watching black shadows on green lawns and red carnations burning in the sun,
Without paying so heavily for it.
That joy and pain, like any mother and her unborn child were almost one.
I could hardly bear
The dreams upon the eyes of white geraniums in the dusk,
The thick, close voice of musk,
The jessamine music on the thin night air,
Or, sometimes, my own hands about me anywhere—
The sight of my own face (for it was lovely then) even the scent of my own hair,
Oh! there was nothing, nothing that did not sweep to the high seat
Of laughing gods, and then blow down and beat
My soul into the highway dust, as hoofs do the dropped roses of the street.
I think my body was my soul,
And when we are made thus
Who shall control
Our hands, our eyes, the wandering passion of our feet,
Who shall teach us
To thrust the world out of our heart; to say, till perhaps in death,
When the race is run,
And it is forced from us with our last breath
"Thy will be done"?
If it is Your will that we should be content with the tame, bloodless things,
As pale as angels smirking by, with folded wings.
Oh! I know Virtue, and the peace it brings!
The temperate, well-worn smile
The one man gives you, when you are evermore his own:

And afterwards the child's, for a little while
With its unknowing and all-seeing eyes
So soon to change, and make you feel how quick
The clock goes round. If one had learned the trick—
(How does one though?) quite early on,
Of long green pastures under placid skies,
One might be walking now with patient truth.
Whatdid we ever care for it, who have asked for youth,
When, oh! my God! this is going or has gone?

There is a portrait of my mother, at nineteen,
With the black spaniel, standing by the garden seat,
The dainty head held high against the painted green
And throwing out the youngest smile, shy, but half haughty and half sweet.
Her picture then: but simply Youth, or simply Spring
To me to-day: a radiance on the wall,
So exquisite, so heart-breaking a thing
Beside the mask that I remember, shrunk and small,
Sapless and lined like a dead leaf,
All that was left of oh! the loveliest face, by time and grief!

And in the glass, last night, I saw a ghost behind my chair—
Yet why remember it, when one can still go moderately gay—?
Or could—with any one of the old crew,
But oh! these boys! the solemn way
They take you, and the things they say— This "I have only as long as you"
When you remind them you are not precisely twenty-two—
Although at heart perhaps—God! if it were
Only the face, only the hair!
If Jim had written to me as he did to-day
A year ago—and now it leaves me cold—
I know what this means, old, old, old!
Et avec ça—mais on a vécu, tout se paie.

That is not always true: there was my Mother—(well at least the dead are free!)
Yoked to the man that Father was; yoked to the woman I am, Monty too;
The little portress at the Convent School, stewing in hell so patiently;
The poor, fair boy who shot himself at Aix. And what of me—and what of me?
But I, I paid for what I had, and they for nothing. No, one cannot see
How it shall be made up to them in some serene eternity.

If there were fifty heavens God could not give us back the child who went or never came;
Here, on our little patch of this great earth, the sun of any darkened day,
Not one of all the starry buds hung on the hawthorn trees of last year's May,
No shadow from the sloping fields of yesterday;
For everyhour they slant across the hedge a different way,
The shadows are never the same.

"Find rest in Him" One knows the parsons' tags—
Back to the fold, across the evening fields, like any flock of baa-ing sheep:
Yes, it may be, when He has shorn, led us to slaughter, torn the bleating soul in us to rags,
For so He giveth His beloved sleep.
Oh! He will take us stripped and done,
Driven into His heart. So we are won:
Then safe, safe are we? in the shelter of His everlasting wings—
I do not envy Him his victories. His arms are full of broken things.

But I shall not be in them. Let Him take
The finer ones, the easier to break.
And they are not gone, yet, for me, the lights, the colours, the perfumes,
Though now they speak rather in sumptuous rooms,
In silks and in gem-like wines;
Here, even, in this corner where my little candle shines
And overhead the lancet-window glows
With golds and crimsons you could almost drink
To know how jewels taste, just as I used to think
There was the scent in every red and yellow rose
Of all the sunsets. But this place is grey,
And much too quiet. No one here
Why, this is awful, this is fear!
Nothing to see, no face,
Nothing to hear except your heart beating in space
As if the world was ended. Dead at last!
Dead soul, dead body, tied together fast.
These to go on with and alone, to the slow end:
No one to sit with, really, or to speak to, friend to friend:
Out of the long procession, black or white or red
Not one left now to say "Still I am here, then see you, dear, lay here your head."
Only the doll's house looking on the Park

The Lost Muse

To-night, all nights, I know, when the man puts the lights out, very dark.
With, upstairs, in the blue and gold box of a room, just the maids' footsteps overhead,
Then utter silence and the empty world—the room—the bed—
The corpse! No, not quite dead, while this cries out in me
But nearly: very soon to be
A handful of forgotten dust—
There must be someone. Christ! there must,
Tell me there will be some one. Who?
If there were no one else, could it be You?

How old was Mary out of whom you cast
So many devils? Was she young or perhaps for years
She had sat staring, with dry eyes, at this and that man going past
Till suddenly she saw You on the steps of Simon's house
And stood and looked at you through tears.
I think she must have known by those
The thing, for what it was that had come to her.
For some of us there is a passion, I suppose
So far from earthly cares and earthly fears
That in its stillness you can hardly stir
Or in its nearness, lift your hand,
So great that you have simply got to stand
Looking at it through tears, through tears.
Then straight from these there broke the kiss,
I think You must have known by this
The thing for what it was, that had come to You:
She did not love You like the rest
It was in her own way, but at the worst, the best,
She gave you something altogether new.
And through it all, from her, no word,
She scarcely saw You, scarcely heard:
Surely You knew when she so touched You with her hair,
Or by the wet cheek lying there,
And while her perfume clung to You from head to feet all through the day
That You can change the things for which we care,
But even You, unless You kill us, not the way.
This, then was peace for her, but passion too.
I wonder was it like a kiss that once I knew
The only one that I would care to take
Into the grave with me, to which if there were afterwards, to wake.

Almost as happy as the carven dead
In some dim chancel lying head by head
We slept with it, but face to face, the whole night through—
One breath, one throbbing quietness, as if the thing behind our lips was endless life,
Lost, as I woke, to hear in the strange earthly dawn, his "Are you there?"
And lie still, listening to the wind outside, among the firs.

So Mary chose the dream of Him for what was left to her of night and day,
It is the only truth: it is the dream in us that neither life nor death nor any other thing can take away:
But if she had not touched Him in the doorway of the dream could she have cared so much?
She was a sinner, we are what we are: the spirit afterwards, but first, the touch.

And He has never shared with me my haunted house beneath the trees
Of Eden and Calvary, with its ghosts that have not any eyes for tears,
And the happier guests who would not see, or if they did, remember these,
Though they lived there a thousand years.
Outside, too gravely looking at me, He seems to stand,
And looking at Him, if my forgotten spirit came
Unwillingly back, what could it claim
Of those calm eyes, that quiet speech,
Breaking like a slow tide upon the beach,
The scarred, not quite human hand?—
Unwillingly back to the burden of old imaginings
When it has learned so long not to think, not to be,
Again, again it would speak as it has spoken to me of things
That I shall not see!

I cannot bear to look at this divinely bent and gracious head:
When I was small I never quite believed that He was dead:
And at the Convent school I used to lie awake in bed
Thinking about His hands. It did not matter what they said,
He was alive to me, so hurt, so hurt! And most of all in Holy Week
When there was no one else to see
I used to think it would not hurt me too, so terribly,
If He had ever seemed to notice me
    Or, if, for once, He would only speak.

Exspecto Resurrectionem

Oh! King who hast the key
Of that dark room,
The last which prisons us but held not Thee,
Thou know'st its gloom.
Dost Thou a little love this one
Shut in to-night,
Young and so piteously alone,
Cold—out of sight?
Thou know'st how hard and bare
The pillow of that new-made narrow bed
Then leave not there
So dear a head!

On the Road to the Sea

We passed each other, turned and stopped for half an hour, then went our way,
I who make other women smile did not make you—
But no man can move mountains in a day.
So this hard thing is yet to do.

But first I want your life:—before I die I want to see
The world that lies behind the strangeness of your eyes,
There is nothing gay or green there for my gathering, it may be,
Yet on brown fields there lies
A haunting purple bloom: is there not something in grey skies
And in grey sea?
I want what world there is behind your eyes,
I want your life and you will not give it me.

Now, if I look, I see you walking down the years,
   Young, and through August fields—a face, a thought, a swinging dream perched on a stile—;
I would have liked (so vile we are!) to have taught you tears
But most to have made you smile.

To-day is not enough or yesterday: God sees it all—
Your length on sunny lawns, the wakeful rainy nights—; tell me—; (how vain to ask),
But it is not a question—just a call—;
Show me then, only your notched inches climbing up the garden wall,
I like you best when you are small.

Is this a stupid thing to say
Not having spent with you one day?
No matter; I shall never touch your hair
Or hear the little tick behind your breast,
Still it is there,
And as a flying bird

Brushes the branches where it may not rest
I have brushed your hand and heard
The child in you: I like that best
So small, so dark, so sweet; and were you also then too grave and wise?
Always I think. Then put your far off little hand in mine ;—Oh! let it rest;
I willnot stare into the early world beyond the opening eyes,
Or vex or scare what I love best.
But I want your life before mine bleeds away—
Here—not in heavenly hereafters—soon
I want your smile this very afternoon,
(The last of all my vices, pleasant people used to say,
I wanted and I sometimes got—the Moon!)

You know, at dusk, the last bird's cry,
And round the house the flap of the bat's low flight,
Trees that go black against the sky
And then—how soon the night!

No shadow of you on any bright road again,
And at the darkening end of this—what voice? whose kiss? As if you'd say!
It is not I who have walked with you, it will not be I who take away
Peace, peace, my little handful of the gleaner's grain
From your reaped fields at the shut of day.

Peace! Would you not rather die
Reeling,—with all the cannons at your ear?
So, at least, would I,
And I may not be here
To-night, to-morrow morning or next year.
Still I willlet you keep your life a little while,
See dear?
I have made you smile.

The Sunlit House

White through the gate it gleamed and slept
In shuttered sunshine: the parched garden flowers
Their fallen petals from the beds unswept,
Like children unloved and ill-kept
Dreamed through the hours.
Twoblue hydrangeas by the blistered door, burned brown,
Watched there and no one in the town
Cared to go past, it night or day,
Though why this was they wouldn't say.
But, I the stranger, knew that I must stay,
Pace up the weed-grown paths and down,
Till one afternoon—there is just a doubt—
But I fancy I heard a tiny shout—
From an upper window a bird flew out—
And I went my way.

The Shade-Catchers

I think they were about as high
As haycocks are. They went running by
Catching bits of shade in the sunny Street:
"I've got one," cried sister to brother,
"I've got two." "Now I've got another."
But scudding away on their little bare feet,
They left the shade in the sunny street.

Le Sacre-Coeur
(Montmartre)

It is dark up here on the heights,
Between the dome and the stars it is quiet too,
While down there under the crowded lights
Flares the importunate face of you,
Dear Paris of the hot white hands, the scarlet lips, the scented hair,
Une jolie file a vendre, ti-es cher;
A thing of gaiety, a thing of sorrow,
Bought to-night, possessed, and tossed
Back to the mart again to-morrow,
Worth and over, what you cost;
While half your charm is that you are
Withal, like some unpurchasable star,
So old, so young and infinite and lost.

It is dark on the dome-capped hill,
Serenely dark, divinely still,
Yet here is the Man who bought you first
Dying of his immortal smart,
Your Lover, the King with the broken heart,
Who while you, feasting, drink your fill,
Pass round the cup
Not looking up,
Calls down to you, "I thirst."

"A king with a broken heart! *Mon Dieu!*
One breaks so many, *cela peut se croire,*
To remember all *c 'est la mer ~ boire,*
And the first, *mais corn me c'est vieux.*
Perhaps there is still some keepsake—or
One has possibly sold it for a song:
Onne peut pas toujours pleurer les rnorts,
And this One—He has been dead so long!"

Song

Love, Love to-day, my dear,
Love is not always here;
Wise maids know how soon grows sere
The greenest leaf of Spring;
But no man knoweth
Whither it goeth
When the wind bloweth
So frail a thing.

Love, Love, my dear, to-day,
If the ship's in the bay,
If the bird has come your way
That sings on summer trees
When his song faileth
And the ship saileth
No voice availeth
To call back these.

Saturday Market

Bury your heart in some deep green hollow
Or hide it up in a kind old tree
Better still, give it the swallow
When she goes over the sea.

In Saturday Market there's eggs a 'plenty
And dead-alive ducks with their legs tied down,
Grey old gaffers and boys of twenty—
Girls and the women of the town—
Pitchers and sugar-sticks, ribbons and laces,
Posies and whips and dicky-birds' seed,
Silver pieces and smiling faces,
In Saturday Market they've all they need.

What were you showing in Saturday Market
That set it grinning from end to end
Girls and gaffers and boys of twenty—?
Cover it close with your shawl, my friend—
Hasten you home with the laugh behind you,
Over the down—, out of sight,
Fasten your door, though no one will find you
No one will look on a Market night.

See, you, the shawl is wet, take out from under
The red dead thing—. In the white of the moon
On the flags does it stir again? Well, and no wonder!
Best make an end of it; bury it soon.
If there is blood on the hearth who'll know it?
Or blood on the stairs,
When a murder is over and done why show it?
In Saturday Market nobody cares.

Then lie you straight on your bed for a short, short weeping

And still, for a long, long rest,
There's never a one in the town so sure of sleeping
As you, in the house on the down with a hole in your breast.

Think no more of the swallow,
Forget, you, the sea,
Never again remember the deep green hollow
Or the top of the kind old tree!

Arracombe Wood

Some said, because he wud'n spaik
Any words to women but Yes and No,
Nor put out his hand for Parson to shake
He mun be bird-witted. But I do go
By the lie of the barley that he did sow,
And I wish no better thing than to hold a rake
Like Dave, in his time, or to see him mow.

Put up in churchyard a month ago,
"A bitter old soul," they said, but it wadn't so.
His heart were in Arracombe Wood where he'd used to go
To sit and talk wi' his shadder till sun went low,
Though what it was all about us'll never know.
And there baint no mem'ry in the place
Of th' old man's footmark, nor his face;
Arracombe Wood do think more of a crow—
'Will be violets there in the Spring: in Summer time the spider's lace;
And come the Fall, the whizzle and race
Of the dry, dead leaves when the wind gies chase;
And on the Eve of Christmas, fallin' snow.

Sea Love

Tide be runnin' the great world over:
T~was only last June month I mind that we
Was thinkin' the toss and the call in the breast of the lover
So everlastjn' as the sea.

Heer's the same little fishes that sputter and swim,
Wi' the moon's old gum on the grey, wet sand;
An' him no more to me nor me to him
Than the wind goin' over my hand.

The Road to Kérity

Do you remember the two old people we passed on the road to Kérity,
Resting their sack on the stones, by the drenched wayside,
Looking at us with their lightless eyes through the driving rain, and then out again
To the rocks, and the long white line of the tide:
Frozen ghosts that were children once, husband and wife, father, and mother,
Looking at us with those frozen eyes; have you ever seen anything quite so chilled or so old?
But we—with our arms about each other,
We did not feel the cold!

I Have Been Through the Gates

His heart, to me, was a place of palaces and pinnacles and shining towers;
I saw it then as we see things in dreams,—I do not remember how long I slept;
I remember the trees, and the high, white walls, and how the sun was always on the towers;
The walls are standing to-day, and the gates: I have been through the gates, I have groped, I have crept
Back, back. There is dust in the streets, and blood; they are empty; darkness is over them;
His heart is a place with the lights gone out, forsaken by great winds and the heavenly rain,
Unclean and unswept,
Like the heart of the holy city, old, blind, beautiful Jerusalem,
Over which Christ wept.

The Cenotaph

Not yet will those measureless fields be green again
Where only yesterday the wild, sweet, blood of wonderful youth was shed;
There is a grave whose earth must hold too long, too deep a stain,
Though for ever over it we may speak as proudly as we may tread.
But here, where the watchers by lonely hearths from the thrust of an inward
Sword have more slowly bled,
We shall build the Cenotaph: Victory, winged, with Peace, winged too, at the column's head.
And over the stairway, at the foot—oh! here, leave desolate, passionate hands to spread
Violets, roses, and laurel, with the small, sweet, twinkling country things
Speaking so wistfully of other Springs,
From the little gardens of little places where son or sweetheart was born and bred.
In splendid sleep, with a thousand brothers
To lovers—to mothers
Here, too, lies he:
Under the purple, the green, the red,
It is all young life: it must break some women's hearts to see
Such a brave, gay coverlet to such a bed!
Only, when all is done and said,
God is not mocked and neither are the dead.

For this will stand in our Market-place— Who'll sell, who'll buy
(Will you or I
Lie each to each with the better grace)?
While looking into every busy whore's and huckster's face
As they drive their bargains, is the Face
Of God: and some young, piteous, murdered face.

In the Fields

Lord, when I look at lovely things which pass,
Under old trees the shadows of young leaves
Dancing to please the wind along the grass,
Or the gold stillness of the August sun on the August sheaves;
Can I believe there is a heavenlier world than this?
And if there is
Will the strange heart of any everlasting thing
Bring me these dreams that take my breath away?
They come at evening with the home-flying rooks and the scent of hay,
Over the fields. They come in Spring.

From a Window

Up here, with June, the sycamore throws
Across the window a whispering screen;
I shall miss the sycamore more, I suppose,
Than anything else on this earth that is out in green.
But I mean to go through the door without fear,
Not caring much what happens here
When I'm away:—
How green the screen is across the panes
Or who goes laughing along the lanes
With my old lover all the summer day.

Not for that City

Not for that city of the level sun,
Its golden streets and glittering gates ablaze—
The shadeless, sleepless city of white days,
White nights, or nights and days that are as one—
We weary, when all is said, all thought, all done.
We strain our eyes beyond this dusk to see
What, from the threshold of eternity
We shall step into. No, I think we shun
The splendour of that everlasting glare,
The clamour of that never-ending song.
And if for anything we greatly long,
It is for some remote and quiet stair
Which winds to silence and a space of sleep
Too sound for waking and for dreams too deep.

Rooms

I remember rooms that have had their part
In the steady slowing down of the heart.
The room in Paris, the room at Geneva,
The little damp room with the seaweed smell,
And that ceaseless maddening sound of the tide—
Rooms where for good or for ill—things died.
But there is the room where we (two) lie dead,
Though every morning we seem to wake and might just as well seem to sleep again
As we shall somewhere in the other quieter, dustier bed
Out there in the sun—in the rain.

Monsieur qui Passe
(Quai Voltaire)

A purple blot against the dead white door
In my friend's rooms, bathed in their vile pink light,
I had not noticed her before
She snatched my eyes and threw them back to me:
She did not speak till we came out into the night,
Paused at this bench beside the kiosk on the quay.

God knows precisely what she said— I left to her the twisted skein,
Though here and there I caught a thread,—
Something, at first, about "the lamps along the Seine,
And Paris, with that witching card of Spring
Kept up her sleeve,—why you could see
The trick done on these freezing winter nights!
While half the kisses of the Quay—
Youth, hope,—the whole enchanted string
Of dreams hung on the Seine's long line of lights."

Then suddenly she stripped, the very skin
Came off her soul,—a mere girl clings
Longer to some last rag, however thin,
When she has shown you—well—all sorts of things:
"If it were daylight—oh! one keeps one's head—
But fourteen years!—No one has ever guessed—
The whole thing starts when one gets to bed—
Death?—If the dead would tell us they had rest!
But your eyes held it as I stood there by the door—
One speaks to Christ—one tries to catch His garment's hem—
One hardly says as much to Him—no more:
It was not you, it was your eyes—I spoke to them."

She stopped like a shot bird that flutters still,
And drops, and tries to run again, and swerves.

The tale should end in some walled house upon a hill.
My eyes, at least, won't play such havoc there,—
Or hers— But she had hair!—blood dipped in gold;
And there she left me throwing back the first odd stare.
Some sort of beauty once, but turning yellow, getting old.
Pouah! These women and their nerves!
God! but the night *is* cold!

Do Dreams Lie Deeper?

His dust looks up to the changing sky
Through daisies' eyes;
And when a swallow flies
Only so high
He hears her going by
As daisies do. He does not die
In this brown earth where he was glad enough to lie.
But looking up from that other bed,
"There is something more my own," he said,
"Than hands or feet or this restless head
That must be buried when I am dead.
The Trumpet may wake every other sleeper.
Do dreams lie deeper—?
And what sunrise
When these are shut shall open their little eyes?
They are my children, they have very lovely faces—
And how does one bury the breathless dreams?
They are not of the earth and not of the sea
They have no friends here but the flakes of the falling snow;
You and I will go down two paces—
Where do they go?"

Domus Caedet Arborem

Ever since the great planes were murdered at the end of the gardens
The city, to me, at night has the look of a Spirit brooding crime;
As if the dark houses watching the trees from dark windows
Were simply biding their time.

Fin de Fête

Sweetheart, for such a day
One mustn't grudge the score;
Here, then, it's all to pay,
It's Good-night at the door.

Good-night and good dreams to you,—
Do you remember the picture-book thieves
Who left two children sleeping in a wood the long night through,
And how the birds came down and covered them with leaves?

So you and I should have slept,—But now,
Oh, what a lonely head!
With just the shadow of a waving bough
In the moonlight over your bed.

Again

One day, not here, you will find a hand
Stretched out to you as you walk down some heavenly street;
You will see a stranger scarred from head to feet;
But when he speaks to you you will not understand,
Nor yet who wounded him nor why his wounds are sweet.
And saying nothing, letting go his hand,
You will leave him in the heavenly street—
So we shall meet!

Epitaph

He loved gay things
Yet with the brave
He laughed when he was covered with grey wings,
—Asking the darkest angel for bright things
And the angel gave—
So with a smile he overstepped the grave.

Friend, Wherefore-?

I will not count the years—there are days too—
And to-night again I have said
"What if you should be lying dead?"
Well, if it were so, I could only lay my head
Quietly on the pillow of my bed
Thinking of Him on whom poor sufferers cried
Suffering Himself so much before He died:
  And then of Judas walking three years by His side—
How Judas kissed Him—how He was crucified.
Always when I see you
I see those two;
Oh! God it is true
We do not, all of us, know what we do;
But Judas knew.

I So Like Spring

I so liked Spring last year
Because you were here;—
The thrushes too—
Because it was these you so liked to hear—
I so liked you.

This year's a different thing,—
I'll not think of you.
But I'll like Spring because it is simply Spring
As the thrushes do.

Here Lies a Prisoner

Leave him: he's quiet enough: and what matter
Out of his body or in, you can scatter
The frozen breath of his silenced soul, of his outraged soul to the winds that rave:
Quieter now than he used to be, but listening still to the magpie chatter
Over his grave.

May, 1915

Let us remember Spring will come again
To the scorched, blackened woods, where the wounded trees
Wait, with their old wise patience for the heavenly rain,
Sureof the sky: sure of the sea to send its healing breeze,
Sure of the sun. And even as to these
Surely the Spring, when God shall please,
Will come again like a divine surprise
To those who sit to-day with their great Dead, hands in their hands, eyes in their eyes,
At one with Love, at one with Grief: blind to the scattered things and changing skies.

June, 1915

Who thinks of June's first rose to-day?
Only some child, perhaps, with shining eyes and rough bright hair will reach it down
In a green sunny lane, to us almost as far away
As are the fearless stars from these veiled lamps of town.
What's little June to a great broken world with eyes gone dim
From too much looking on the face of grief, the face of dread?
Or what's the broken world to June and him
Of the small eager hand, the shining eyes, the rough bright head?

Ne Me Tangeto

"This man... would have known who and what manner of woman this is: for she is a sinner.
"—S. Luke *vii. 39.*

Odd, *You* should fear the touch,
The first that I was ever ready to let go,
I, that have not cared much
For any toy I could not break and throw
To the four winds when I had done with it. You need not fear the touch,
Blindest of all the things that I have cared for very much
In the whole gay, unbearable, amazing show.

True—for a moment—no, dull heart, you were too small,
Thinking to hide the ugly doubt behind that hurried puzzled little smile:
Only the shade, was it, you saw? but still the shade of something vile:
Oddest of all!
So I will tell you this. Last night, in sleep,
Walking through April fields I heard the far-off bleat of sheep
And from the trees about the farm, not very high,
A flight of pigeons fluttered up into an early evening mackerel sky;
Someone stood by and it was you:
About us both a great wind blew.
My breast was bared
But sheltered by my hair
I found you, suddenly, lying there,
Tugging with tiny fingers at my heart, no more afraid:
The weakest thing, the most divine
That ever yet was mine,
Something that I had strangely made,
So then it seemed—
The child for which I had not looked or ever cared,
    Of whom, before, I had never dreamed.

Old Shepherd's Prayer

Up to the bed by the window, where I be lyin',
Comes bells and bleat of the flock wi' they two children's clack.
Over, from under the eaves there's the starlings flyin',
And down in yard, fit to burst his chain, yapping out at Sue I do hear young Mac.

Turning around like a falled-over sack
   I can see team ploughin' in Whithy-bush field and meal carts startin' up road to Church-Town;
Saturday arternoon the men goin' back
And the women from market, trapin' home over the down.

Heavenly Master, I wud like to wake to they same green places
Where I be know'd for breakin' dogs and follerin' sheep.
And if I may not walk in th' old ways and look on th' old faces
I wud sooner sleep.

My Heart Is Lame

My heart is lame with running after yours so fast
Such a long way,
Shall we walk slowly home, looking at all the things we passed
Perhaps to-day?

Home down the quiet evening roads under the quiet skies,
Not saying much,
You for a moment giving me your eyes
When you could bear my touch.
But not to-morrow. This has taken all my breath;
Then, though you look the same,
There may be something lovelier in Love's face in death
As your heart sees it, running back the way we came;
My heart is lame.

On Youth Struck Down
(From an unfinished elegy)

Oh! Death what have you to say?
"Like a bride—like a bride-groom they ride away:
You shall go back to make up the fire,
To learn patience—to learn grief,
To learn sleep when the light has quite gone out of your earthly skies,
But they have the light in their eyes
To the end of their day."

The Rambling Sailor

In the old back streets o' Pimlico,
On the docks at Monte Video,
At the Ring o' Bells on Plymouth Hoe
He'm arter me now wheerever I go.
An' dirty nights when the wind do blow
I can hear him sing-songin' up from sea:
Oh! no man nor woman's bin friend to me
An' to-day I'm feared wheer to-morrow I'll be,
Sin' the night the moon lay whist and white
On the road goin' down to the Lizard Light
When I heard him hummin' behind me.

"Oh! look, boy, look in your sweetheart's eyes
So deep as sea an 'so blue as skies;
An' 'tis better to kiss than to chide her.
If they tell 'ee no tales, they 'Ii tell 'ee no lies
Of the little brown mouse
That creeps into the house
To lie sleepin 'so quiet beside her.

"Oh! hold 'ee long, but hold 'ee light
Your true man's hand when you find him,
He'll help 'ee home on a darksome night
Wi' a somethin' bright
That he 'm holdin' tight
In the hand that he keeps behind him.

"Oh! sit 'ee down to your whack o'pies,
So hot's the stew and the brew likewise,
But whiles you 'm scra pin' the plates and dishes,
A 'gapin 'down in the shiversome sea
For the delicate mossels inside o 'we
Theer's a passel o 'hungry fishes."

At the *Halte des Marins* at *Saint Nazaire*
I cussed him, sittin' astride his chair;
An' Christmas Eve on the Mary Clare
I pitched him a'down the hatch-way stair.
But "Shoutin' and cloutin's nothing to me,
Nor the hop nor the skip nor the jump," says he,
"For I be walkin' on every quay—
"So look, boy, look in the dear maid's eyes
And take the true man's hand
And eat your fill o 'your whack o 'pies
Till you 'm starin' up wheer the sea-crow flies
Wi 'your head lyin'soft in the sand."

The Call

From our low seat beside the fire
Where we have dozed and dreamed and watched the glow
Or raked the ashes, stopping so
We scarcely saw the sun or rain
Above, or looked much higher
Than this same quiet red or burned-out fire.
To-night we heard a call,
A rattle on the window-pane,
A voice on the sharp air,
And felt a breath stirring our hair,
A flame within us: Something swift and tall
Swept in and out and that was all.
Was it a bright or a dark angel? Who can know?
It left no mark upon the snow,
But suddenly it snapped the chain
Unbarred, flung wide the door
Which will not shut again;
And so we cannot sit here any more.
We must arise and go:
The world is cold without
And dark and hedged about
With mystery and enmity and doubt,
But we must go
Though yet we do not know
Who called, or what marks we shall leave upon the snow.

Absence

Sometimes I know the way
You walk, up over the bay;
It is a wind from that far sea
That blows the fragrance of your hair to me.

Or in this garden when the breeze
Touches my trees
To stir their dreaming shadows on the grass
I see you pass.

In sheltered beds, the heart of every rose
Serenely sleeps to-night. As shut as those
Your guarded heart; as safe as they from the beat, beat
Of hooves that tread dropped roses in the street.

Turn never again
On these eyes blind with a wild rain
Your eyes; they were stars to me.—
There are things stars may not see.

But call, call, and though Christ stands
Still with scarred hands
Over my mouth, I must answer. So
I will come—He shall let me go!

The Trees Are Down

—and he cried with a loud voice:
Hurt not the earth, neither the sea, nor the trees— (Revelation.)

They are cutting down the great plane-trees at the end of the gardens.
For days there has been the grate of the saw, the swish of the branches as they fall,
The crash of the trunks, the rustle of trodden leaves,
With the "Whoops" and the "Whoas," the loud common talk, the loud common laughs of the men, above it all.

I remember one evening of a long past Spring
Turning in at a gate, getting out of a cart, and finding a large dead rat in the mud of the drive.
I remember thinking: alive or dead, a rat was a god-forsaken thing, But at least, in May, that even a rat should be alive.

The week's work here is as good as done. There is just one bough
On the roped bole, in the fine grey rain,
Green and high
And lonely against the sky.
(Down now!—)
And but for that,
If an old dead rat
Did once, for a moment, unmake the Spring, I might never have thought of him again.

It is not for a moment the Spring is unmade to-day;
These were great trees, it was in them from root to stem:
When the men with the "Whoops" and the "Whoas" have carted the whole of the whispering loveliness away
Half the Spring, for me, will have gone with them.

It is going now, and my heart has been struck with the hearts of the planes;
Half my life it has beat with these, in the sun, in the rains,
In the March wind, the May breeze,
In thegreat gales that came over to them across the roofs from the great seas.
There was only a quiet rain when they were dying;
They must have heard the sparrows flying,
And the small creeping creatures in the earth where they were lying—
But I, all day, I heard an angel crying:
  "Hurt not the trees."

Smile Death

Smile, Death, see I smile as I come to you
Straight from the road and the moor that I leave behind,
Nothing on earth to me was like this wind-blown space,
Nothing was like the road, but at the end there was a vision or a face
And the eyes were not always kind.

Smile, Death, as you fasten the blades to my feet for me,
On, on let us skate past the sleeping willows dusted with snow;
Fast, fast down the frozen stream, with the moor and the road and the vision behind,
(Show me your face, why the eyes are kind!)
And we will not speak of life or believe in it or remember it as we go.

To a Child in Death

You would have scoffed if we had told you yesterday
Love made us feel, or so it was with me, like some great bird
Trying to hold and shelter you in its strong wing;—
A gay little shadowy smile would have tossed us back such a solemn word,
And it was not for that you were listening
When so quietly you slipped away
With half the music of the world unheard.
What shall we do with this strange summer, meant for you,—
Dear, if we see the winter through
What shall be done with spring?
This, this is the victory of the Grave; here is death's sting,
That it is not strong enough, our strongest wing.

But what of His who like a Father pitieth?
His Son was also, once, a little thing,
The wistfullest child that ever drew breath,
Chased by a sword from Bethlehem and in the busy house at Nazareth
Playing with little rows of nails, watching the carpenter's hammer swing,
Long years before His hands and feet were tied
And by a hammer and the three great nails He died,
Of youth, of Spring,
Of sorrow, of loneliness, of victory the King,
Under the shadow of that wing.

Moorland Night

My face is against the grass—the moorland grass is wet—
My eyes are shut against the grass, against my lips there are the little blades,
Over my head the curlews call,
And now there is the night wind in my hair;
My heart is against the grass and the sweet earth ;—it has gone still, at last.
It does not want to beat any more,
And why should it beat?
This is the end of the journey;
The Thing is found.

This is the end of all the roads—
Over the grass there is the night-dew
And the wind that drives up from the sea along the moorland road;
I hear a curlew start out from the heath
And fly off, calling through the dusk,
The wild, long, rippling call.
The Thing is found and I am quiet with the earth.
Perhaps the earth will hold it, or the wind, or that bird's cry,
But it is not for long in any life I know. This cannot stay,
Not now, not yet, not in a dying world, with me, for very long.
I leave it here:
And one day the wet grass may give it back—
One day the quiet earth may give it back—
The calling birds may give it back as they go by—
To someone walking on the moor who starves for love and will not know
Who gave it to all these to give away;
Or, if I come and ask for it again,
Oh! then, to me.

An Ending

You know that road beside the sea,
Walled by the wavin' wheat,
Which winds down to the little town,
Wind-blown and gray and up the crooked Street?
We'd used to meet
Just at the top, and when the grass was trodden down
'Twas by our feet.
We'd used to stand
And watch the clouds like a great fleet
Sail over sea and over land
And the gulls dart
Above our heads: and by the gate
At the road's end, when et was late
And all the ships was showing lights on quiet nights,
We'd used to part.

So, Sir, you think I've missed my way,
There's nothing but the Judgment Seat—
But ef I pray perhaps I may—what's that you say—
A golden street?
Give me the yellow wheat!
Et edn't *there* we'm goin' to meet!
No, I'm not mazed, I make no doubt
That ef we don't my soul goes out
'Most like a candle in the everlasting dark.
And what's the odds? 'Twas just a spark
Alight for her.
I tell you, Sir,
That God He made et brave and plain,
Sin' He knows better than yon Book
What's in a look
You'd go to Hell to get again.
Another hour? An hour to wait—!

I sim I'll meet her at the gate—
You know that road beside the sea—
The crooked street—the wavin' wheat—?
(What's that? A lamp! Et made me start—)
That's where our feet—we'd used to meet—on quiet nights—
My God! the ships es showing lights!—
We'd used—to part.

A Question

If Christ was crucified—Ah! God, are we
Not scourged, tormented, mocked and called to pay
The sin of ages in our little day—
Has man no crown of thorns, no Calvary,
Though Christ has tasted of his agony?
We knew no Eden and the poisoned fruit
We did not pluck, yet from the bitter root
We sprang, maimed branches of iniquity.

Have we who share the heritage accurst
Wrought nothing? Tainted to the end of time,
The last frail souls still suffer for the first
Blind victims of an everlasting crime.
Ask of the Crucified, Who hangs enthroned,
If man—oh! God, man too has not atoned.

Left Behind

Wilt thou have pity? intercede for me.
So near, at last thou standest to the throne,
Thou mayest call for mercy on thine own,
As here thine own for mercy calls on thee.
Fling then my soul, thy soul, upon its knee;
Bestir these lips of mine for me to pray;
Release this spirit from its tortured clay,
Remembering that thine, its mate, is free.

I wait thy summons on a swaying floor,
Within a room half darkness and half glare.
I cannot stir—I cannot find the stair—
Thrust hands upon my heart—; it clogs my feet,
As drop by drop it drains. I stand and beat—
I stand and beat my heart against the door.

A Farewell

Remember me and smile, as smiling too,
I have remembered things that went their way—
The dolls with which I grew too wise to play—
Or over-wise—and kissed, as children do,
And so dismissed them; yes, even as you
Have done with this poor piece of painted clay—
Not wantonly, but wisely, shall we say?
As one who, haply, tunes his heart anew.

Only I wish her eyes may not be blue,
The eyes of the new angel. Ah! she may
Miss something that I found,—perhaps the clue
To those long silences of yours, which grew
Into one word. And should she not be gay,
Poor lady! Well, she too must have her day.

"There Shall Be No Night There"
(In the Fields)

Across these wind-blown meadows I can see
The far off glimmer of the little town
And feel the darkness slowly shutting down
To lock from day's long glare my soul and me.
Then through my blood the coming mystery
of night steals to my heart and turns my feet
Toward that chamber in the lamp-lit street.
Where waits the pillow of thy breast and thee.

"There shall be no night there" —no curtained pane
To shroud love's speechlessness and loose thy hair
For kisses swift and sweet as falling rain.
No soft release of life—no evening prayer.
Nor shall we waking greet the dawn, aware
That with the darkness we may sleep again.

V.R.I.

I. *January 22nd, 1901*
'A Nation's Sorrow.' No. In that strange hour
We did but note the flagging pulse of day,
The sudden pause of Time, and turn away
Incredulous of grief; beyond the power
Of question or of tears. Thy people's pain
Was their perplexity: Thou could'st not be
God's and not England's. Let Thy spirit reign,
For England is not England without Thee.
Still Thine, Immortal Dead, she still shall stake
Thy fame against the world, and hold supreme
Thy unsuspended sway. Then lay not down
Thy sceptre, lest her Empire prove a dream
Of Thine, great, gentle Sleeper, who shalt wake
When God doth please, to claim another crown.

II. *February 2nd, 1901*
When, wrapped in the calm majesty of sleep,
She passes through her people to her rest,
Has she no smile in slumber? Is her breast,
Even to their sorrow, pulseless? Shall they weep
And She not with them? Nothing is so strange
As this, that England's passion, be it pain,
Or joy, or triumph, never shall again
Find voice in her. No change is like this change.
For all this mute indifference of death,
More dear She is than She has ever been.
The dark crowd gathers: not 'The Queen! The Queen!'
Upon its lips to-day. A quickened breath—
She passes—through the hush, the straining gaze,
The vast, sweet silence of its love and praise.

To a Little Child in Death

Dear, if little feet make little journeys,
Thine should not be far;
Though beyond the faintest star,
Past earth's last bar,
Where angels are,
Thou hast to travel—
Cross the far blue spaces of the sea,
Climb above the tallest tree,
Higher up than many mountains be;
Sure there is some shorter way for thee,
Since little feet make little journeys.

Then, if smallest limbs are soonest weary,
Thou should'st soon be there;
Stumbling up the golden stair,
Where the angels' shining hair
Brushes dust from baby faces.
Very, very gently cling
To a silver-edged wing,
And peep from under.
Then thou'lt see the King,
Then will many voices sing,
And thou wilt wonder.
Wait a little while
For Him to smile,
Who calleth thee.
 He who calleth all,
Both great and small,
From over mountain, star and sea,
Doth call the smallest soonest to His knee,
Since smallest limbs are soonest weary.

Peri en Mer
(Camaret)

One day the friends who stand about my bed
Will slowly turn from it to speak of me
Indulgently, as of the newly dead,
Not knowing how I perished by the sea,
That night in summer when the gulls topped white
The crowded masts cut black against a sky
Of fading rose—where suddenly the light
Of Youth went out, and I, no longer I,
Climbed home, the homeless ghost I was to be.
Yet as I passed, they sped me up the heights—
Old seamen round the door of the Abri
De la Tempête. Even on quiet nights
So may some ship go down with all her lights
Beyond the sight of watchers on the quay!

Unpublished Poems

These four previously unpublished poems by Charlotte Mew were discovered in typescript with her signature in the collection of Jean Hersholt together with an inscribed copy of The Farmer's Bride. Charlotte was known to have destroyed probably the majority of her work prior to her death and it can be assumed that these poems were intended to be included in a first edition of her only (at that point in time) published book of poetry. It is also possible that these poems were excluded by Harold Monro from the poems she submitted to The Poetry Bookshop. The manuscripts were likely left with Monro who then enclosed them in a copy of the published book for reasons unknown. The poems are untitled and the numbers are provided only as a means of identification. They are in no particular order and only guesswork could be employed to arrive at a date for their composition.

I.

You told me to wait
But I did not.
You told me to seek another
But I did not.
You tell me to forget
And still I try
And see no way of living
but to die.

II.

Those leaves on the silver birch
Shimmer the way I did
When you said you loved me.
They shimmer still in the autumn breeze;
They are merely leaves.
But I
Cannot shimmer
As is my due
Without you.

III.

Men say an owl can see in night's dread dark
That it can find a wind where none can be.
But I must dream you in the river's calm
And know that in the night, I cannot see.

IV.

When I ran away from you and saw that all was new
I, like Lot's wife,
looked back.
But, ah, there all similarities end,
For I was not in the Holy Land
And, alas, I could not see
nor saw
Even your shadow on the empty road
And if I refused to halt
Perhaps to reconsider
My lot was bitter.
I did not turn to salt.

Charlotte Mew: A Selected Bibliography in Print

Bishop, J. Dean. Ascent into Nothingness: The Poetry of Charlotte Mew. Diss. LSU, ;1968.

Blunt, Wilfrid. Cockerell. New York: Knopf, 1965.

Boll, Theophilus E. M. Miss May Sinclair: Novelist. Rutherford: Fairleigh Dickinson Univ. Press, 1973.

---. "The Mystery of Charlotte Mew and May Sinclair: An Inquiry." Bulletin of the New York Public Library 74 (1970): 445-53

Catty, Charles. "Song of Sorrow." Poem. The Yellow Book IX (Apr. 1896): 157.

---. "The Wind in the Tree." Poem. The Yellow Book XI (Oct 1896): 283.

Chesson, W. H. Rev. of The Farmer's Bride. The Bookman July 1921: 181.

Childe, Wilfred Rowland. Rev.of The Farmer's Bride. Voices May1921: 92

Cockerell, Sydney C. "Miss Charlotte Mew: A Poet of Rare Quality." Obituary. The Times 29 March 1928: 21a.

Collard, Lorna Reeling. "Charlotte Mew." Contemporary Review 137 (Apr 1930): 501-08.

Corke, Hilary. "Absence in Reality." Encounter June 1954- 74-81.

Crisp, Shelley Jean. The Woman Poet Emerges: The Literary Tradition of Mary Coleridge, Alice Meynell, and Charlotte Mew. Diss. Univ. of Massachusetts, 1987. Ann Arbor: UMI, 1987. DA8710440.

Davidow, Mary C. "Charlotte Mew and the Shadow of Thomas Hardy." Bulletin of Research in the Humanities 81 (1978): 437-447.

---. Charlotte Mew: Biography and Criticism. Diss. Brown Univ.,1960. Ann Arbor: UMI, 1963. 62-5740.

---. "The Charlotte Mew-May Sinclair Relationship: Reply." Bulletin of the New York Public Library 75 (1971: 295-300.

---. "The Christminster Mystique and the Immanent Will in Jude the Obscure." Christianity and Literature 23.2 (19741: 28-

Deutsch, Babette. Poetry in Our Time: A Critical Survey of Poetry in the English-Speaking World. 1900 to 1960. New York. Doubleday, 1963.

Dickinson, Patric. "A Note on Charlotte Mew." The Nineteenth Century and After July 1948: 42-47.

Doolittle, Hilda. Rev.of The Farmer's Bride. The Egoist Sept 1916: 135.

"Emotion in Restraint." The Times Literary Supplement 18 Dec. 1953: 814.

Fairchild, Hoxie Neale. Religious Trends in English Poetry: Gods of a Changing Poetry.

New York: Columbia; Univ. Press, 1962.

    Rev. of The Farmer's Bride, by Charlotte Mew. Nation 27 July 1921: 104.

    Feaver, Vicki. "Managing the Unmanageable." Rev. of Charlotte Mew: Poems and Prose, ed. Val Warner. Times Literary Supplement 4 Dec. 1981: 1413-14.

    Freeman, John. "Charlotte Mew." The Bookman June 1929: 1413-46.

    Fitzgerald, Penelope. Charlotte Mew and Her Friends. New York: Addison Wesley, 1988.

    ---. "Lotti's Leap." Rev. of Collected Poems and ProseLondon Review of Books. 1-14 July 1982: 15-16.

    Gittings, Robert. Thomas Hardy's Later Years. Boston: Little, Brown, 1978.

    --- with Jo Manton. The Second Mrs. Hardy. London: Oxford Univ. Press, 1979.

    Gould, Gerald. Article on Mew. The Bookman Dec 1921: 138-41.

    ---. "The New Poetry. The Bookman August August 1923.

    Grant, Joy. Harold Monro and the Poetry Bookshop. Berkeley: Univ. of California Press, 1967.

    Gutin, Stanley Samuel. The Poems of Charlotte Mew: A Critical Study. College Park, Maryland: Univ. of Maryland Press ?, 1956.

    Hammick, Georgina, ed. Love and Loss: Stories of the Heart. Boston: Faber and Faber, 1992.

    Hardwick, Ann. Voice from the Garden: Aspects of Women's Poetry, 1910-1939. Diss. Univ. of Loughborough(U.K.3, 1988. Ann Arbor: UMI, 1990. BRDX8921.

    Haughton, Hugh. Rev. of Charlotte Mew and Her Friends. London Times Literary Supplement 19 Oct. 1984, 1190.

    Holmes, John. "NA Longer View." Rev. of Collected Poems of Charlotte Mew. Poetry 86.4 (July 1955): 240-241.

    Holroyd, Michael. "Said the be a Writer" in Unreceived Opinions. New York: Holt, Rinehart and Winston, 1974. 153-60.

    Joiner, Sandra Carol. Charlotte Mew: An Introduction. Bowling Green: Western Kentucky Univ., 1989.

    Jones, James John. The Triumphant Victim: Charlotte Mew and the Themes of Division and Degeneration in Late-Victorian Literature. Lawrence: Univ. of Kansas, 1987.

    Knox, E. V. "The Circus Clown." Punch 24 August 1921: 146.

"Two Shepherds." Punch 20 July 1921: 46.

    Leighton, Angela. Victorian Women Poets: Writing Against the Heart. Charlottesville: Univ. of Virginia Press, 1992.

    Leithauser, Brad. "Small Wonder." The New York Review of Books. 15 Jan. 1987: 25-26, 31.

Mew, Charlotte. "At the Convent Gate." Temple Bar CXXV (1902): 299.
    44a --"The Cenotaph." Westminster Gazette 7 September 1919.
---. "The Changeling." The Englishwoman 17 February 1913: 134-136.
---. "The China Bowl." Temple Bar CXVIII (189g9): 64-90: rpt. Living Age CCXXIII (1899): 294-304, 384-393.
---. Collected Poems of Charlotte Mew. London: Duckworth, l953.
---. "The Country Sunday." Temple Bar CXXXII (1905): 598-600.
---. "Exspecto Ressurectionem." Living Age 22 March 1913: 706.
---. "Fame." The New Weekly 30 May 1914: 334.
---. "The Farmer's Bride." The Nation 3 February 1912: 747.
---. The Farmer's Bride. London: Poetry Bookshop, 1916.
---. "A Fatal Fidelity." Cornhill Magazine Autumn, 1953.
---. "The Fete." The Egoist 1 May, l914.
---. "Fin de Fete." The Sphere 17 February l923.
---. "The Governess in Fiction." The Academy 12 August 1899: 163-164.
---. "The Hay-Market." The New Statesman 14 February 1914: 595-597.
---. "Passed." Yellowbook II (July 1894): 121-141.
---. "Pecheresse." The New Weekly 25 July l914: 174.
---. "The Pedlar." The Englishwoman XXI (February 1914): 160.
---. "Peri en Mer." The Englishwoman XX (November 1913): 136.
---. "The Rambling Sailor." The Chapbook (February l922); Literary Digest 1 April 1922: 38: The Bookman LVII (June 1923): 423-423.
---. The Rambling Sailor. London: Poetry Bookshop, 1929.
---. Saturday Market. New York: Macmillan, l921.
---. "Sea Love." The Chapbook (July 1919): 32.
---. "The Smile" Theosophist 8 May 1914: 274-282.
---. "Song." Literary Digest 17 January 1920.
---. "Song: Love, Love To-day." The Athenaeum 24 October 1919: 1058.
---. "Song: Oh! Sorrow, Sorrow." Temple Bar CXXVI (1902): 230.
---. "Sunlit House." The Bookman LXXIV (May 1928): 112-113.
---. "To a Child in Death." Temple Bar LV (April 1922): 117.
---. "The Trees Are Down." The Chapbook (January 1923).
---. "V.R.I." Temple Bar CXXVII (1901): 289-290.
---. "The Voice." The Englishwoman (March 1912): 304.
---. "The Wheat." Time and Tide. 20 February 1954: 237-238.
---. "A White Night." Temple Bar CXXVII (1903): 625-639.
Meynell, Viola, ed. The Best of Friends: Further Letters to Sydney Carlyle Cockerell.

London: Hart-Davis, 1956.

---. Friends of a Lifetime: Letters to Sydney Carlyle Cockerell. London: Jonathan Cape, 1940.

Mizejewski, Linda. "Charlotte Mew and the Unrepentant Magdalene: A Myth in Transition." Texas Studies in Literature and Language 26.3 (1984): 282-302.

Monro, Alida. "Charlotte Mew: A Memoir." In Collected Poems of Charlotte Mew by Charlotte Mew. London: Duckworth, 1953. vii-xx.

Monro, Harold. "Charlotte Mew." The Bookman May 8 1928: 112-113.

---. Twentieth Century Poetry. St. Clair Shores, Mich.: Scholarly Press, 1977.

---. Some Contemporary Poets. London: Leonard Parsons, 1920.

Moore, Virginia. "Charlotte Mew" in "Letters and Comment," Yale Review 22.2 (Dee 1932). 429-30.

---. Distinguished Women Writers. New York: E. P. Dutton, 1934.

Moult, Thomas. "Four Women Poets." The Bookman LXV1924):196-199.

"New Poetry." Rev. of Saturday Market, by Charlotte Mew. New Statesman 2 April 1921: 759.

Oosthuizen, Ann, ed. Stepping Out: Short Stories on Friendship Between Women. London: Pandora Press, 1986.

"The Poems of Charlotte Mew." Rev. of Saturday Market. New York Evening Post, 23 July 1921.

"Poetry." Rev. of The Farmer's Bride, by Charlotte Mew. Times Literary Supplement 21 Sept. 1916 :455.

Rickword, Edgell. Essays and Opinions 1921-1931. Ed. Alan Young. Cheadle, Cheshire: Carcanet,1974

Robertson, David A. "Contemporary English Poets: Charlotte Mew," English Journal XV (May 1926):334-347.

Romily, Giles. Rev. of Collected Poems of Charlotte Mew. The Observer 31, January 1954.

Sackville, Lady Margaret. "Mew." The Bookman LX (Dec 1921): 138.

Schmidt, Michael. A Reader's Guide to Fifty Modern British Poets. New York: Barnes & Noble, 1979. [57-63]

Sitwell, Edith. Rev. of The Farmer's Bride. The Daily Herald 4 April 1921.

---. Time and Tide 21 June 1919: 755-756.

Smith, Joan, ed. Femmes de Siecle: Stories from the '90s: Women Writing at the End of Two Centuries. London: Chatto and Windus, 1992.

Strobel, Marion. Rev. of Saturday Market. Poetry XX June 1922: 152-155.

99a. Swinnerton, Frank. The Georgian Literary Scene 1910-1935. London: J. M.

Dent, 1938. [259-260]

---. The Georgian Scene: A Literary Panorama. New York: Farrar & Rinehart, 1934.

---Two Women Poets. H Rev. of Saturday Market, by Charlotte Mew. The Bookman (London) 54 (Sept. 1921):66.

Untermeyer, Louis. Lives of the Poets. New York: Simon and Schuster, 1959.

---. "The Poems of Charlotte Mew." Literary Review 23 July 1921:

Warner, Val, ed. Charlotte Mew: Collected Poems and Prose. London: Virago, 1981.

---. "Mary Magdalene and the Bride: The Work of Charlotte Mew." Poetry Nation 4 (1975): 92-106.

Watts, Marjorie. "Memories of Charlotte Mew." PEN Broadsheet 13 (Autumn 1982): 12-13.

Wilkinson, Marguerite. "Lyrics That Are Not for Pollyanna." New York Times Book Review 19 June 1921: 10.

Williams-Ellis, A. An Anatomy of Poetry. Oxford: Basil Blackwell, 1922.

Wolfe, Humbert. Rev. of The Rambling Sailor. The Observer (London) 12 June 1929.

INDEX

A Farewell	121
A Note on the Text	23
A Question	119
A Quoi Bon Dire	59
Absence	111
Afternoon Tea	36
Again	97
An Ending	117
Arracombe Wood	83
At The Convent Gate	31
Beside the Bed	46
Bibliography	129
Do Dreams Lie Deeper?	94
Domus Caedet Arborem	95
Epitaph	98
Exspecto Resurrectionem	74
Fame	39
Fin de Fête	96
Friend, Wherefore-?	99
From a Window	89
Here Lies a Prisoner	101
I Have Been Through the Gates	86
I So Like Spring	100
In Nunhead Cemetery	47
In the Fields	88
Introduction	13
Jour des Mortes	64
June, 1915	103
Ken	56
Le Sacre-Coeur	79
Left Behind	120
Madeleine in Church	68
May, 1915	102
Monsieur qui Passe	92
Moorland Night	116
My Heart Is Lame	106
Ne Me Tangeto	104

Not for that City...90
Old Shepherd's Prayer..105
On the Asylum Road..63
On the Road to the Sea..75
On Youth Struck Down...107
Pecheresse..51
Peri en Mer..125
Requiescat...32
Rooms..91
Saturday Market..81
Sea Love..84
She Was A Sinner..37
Smile Death..114
Song of Sorrow...27
Song..80
Song..38
The Call..110
The Cenotaph...87
The Changeling..53
The Farmer's Bride...29
The Fête..41
The Forest Road..65
The Little Portress..34
The Narrow Door...40
The Pedlar...50
The Quiet House..60
The Rambling Sailor..108
The Road to Kérity...85
The Shade-Catchers..78
The Sunlit House..77
The Trees Are Down..112
The Wind and the Tree..28
"There Shall Be No Night There"....................................122
To a Child in Death...115
To a Little Child in Death...124
Unpublished Poems...127
V.R.I...123

Printed in Great Britain
by Amazon